MOST LIKELY TO
SUCCEED AT WORK

ALSO BY WILMA DAVIDSON. Ed.D.

Business Writing: What Works, What Won't

Writing a Winning College Application Essay
(with Susan McCloskey, Ph.D.)

MOST LIKELY TO SUCCEED AT WORK

HOW TO GET AHEAD AT WORK USING EVERYTHING YOU LEARNED IN HIGH SCHOOL

WILMA DAVIDSON, Ed.D.,
AND JACK DOUGHERTY

ST. MARTIN'S GRIFFIN ≉ NEW YORK

www.stmartins.com

Book design by Nick Wunder

Library of Congress Cataloging-in-Publication Data

Davidson, Wilma.
   Most likely to succeed at work : how to get ahead at work using everything
you learned in high school / Wilma Davidson and Jack Dougherty.
      p.   cm.
   ISBN 0-312-31708-5 (hc)
   ISBN 0-312-31709-3 (pbk)
   EAN 978-0312-31709-6
   1. Office politics.   2. Interpersonal relations.   I. Dougherty, Jack   II. Title.

HF5386.5.D38 2003
650.1'3—dc21

2003043119

First St. Martin's Griffin Edition: November 2004

10 9 8 7 6 5 4 3 2 1

FROM WILMA DAVIDSON

For my high school sweetheart

FROM JACK DOUGHERTY

For my mother

CONTENTS

PART ONE: THE CLASS

PART TWO: GETTING TO THE NEXT GRADE LEVEL: ADDITIONAL LESSONS ON ORGANIZATIONAL SURVIVAL

ACKNOWLEDGMENTS

This book, like most, boasts deep and humble origins.

The first debt owed is to our corporate families. The book's inception can be broadly traced to the work we've done over the past couple of decades helping companies, corporate executives, and employees solidify and enhance their reputations. As we wrote the book, we rediscovered that the overwhelming majority of the American workforce, and the people we've worked with, are in the "top of the class." With great respect, we are thankful for the business friendships we've made.

Second, we thank our publishing family. From the beginning, St. Martin's Press showed tremendous enthusiasm and excitement for this book. We are especially grateful to our editor, Marian Lizzi, for her apt advice and talent.

Next, thanks to our real families for their responses to our drafts and for their unconditional love and support.

Last, we thank each other—publicly. When we met in the early 1990s, we became fast friends. By the century's end we lost touch. Luckily, we reconnected. It's tempting to lie and report that during our first conversation in years we had a spirited debate about Aristotle's *Rhetoric*. But the truth is, we joked, reminisced, caught up. Our co-authoring began the moment one of us said, "You know, it's the same *everywhere*—work is just the adult version of high school!" And our collaboration is proof that diverse archetypes can—and do—work productively together.

PREFACE

If you're like most people, you want to go to work, do your job, have some fun, be well paid, be recognized for being good at it, and go home smiling at the end of the day. On the best days, you get all these things, and the experience of work is richly rewarding.

But on the worst days, you go home disappointed, disillusioned, furious, insulted, scared, scarred, and paranoid. Over dinner with your spouse or drinks with your friends, you moan about the office brown-noser who so shamelessly tried to look smart in front of the boss at the staff meeting. Or you gossip about the hot-and-heavy couple in Accounting who are married (though not to each other). Or you complain that you have tried 150 different ways to get the boss's attention, but it is as though you don't exist.

Every day exasperated workers wonder how they will survive the politics and personalities of the modern workplace. It's very exhausting, very stressful, and very real.

Fortunately, survival is a lot easier than you might think. In fact, you may be surprised to learn that you have *already* navigated an equally stressful and complex organizational structure: high school.

As you strive to increase your success in the workplace (to get along, noticed, and promoted), look back to your high school days for insight, clues, and answers about what worked, what didn't, and why. The deeper you dig into your high school past, the more you'll discover that work is simply high school for grown-ups.

INTRODUCTION

THE PREMISE OF THE BOOK

High school is never over.

The workplace—whether a high-rise office building, factory floor, or retail store—is really just an adult version of high school, though many of us pretend otherwise. Look around. The Class President is in the corner office. The Party Animal is out entertaining clients. The Class Clown is in the cafeteria doing a wicked imitation of the Class President. The Gossip is busy telling everyone within earshot the skinny on the controller's divorce proceedings. And the Player just accepted the regional vice president's invitation for drinks after work.

Whether we work on the assembly line or in the executive suite, adults in the workplace gossip, admire, mock, backstab, envy, flatter, covet, cajole, charm, pass notes during meetings, and otherwise behave just as we did in high school. High school is simply a lab for the rest of our life. (Talk about a permanent record!)

Bottom Line

We are who we were in high school, whether we realize it or not. During those years, a mini-adult version of us emerged. Many of the core traits on display then inform our personality and behavior at work today: our ability to make friends easily, or our love of clothes, or our competitive streak, or our willingness to pitch in, or possibly our persistent anger at not being taken seriously. We developed a communication style then—a way of presenting ourselves to the world—and that style is either working for us today or it isn't.

THE PROMISE OF THIS BOOK: HOW IT CAN HELP YOU

You were typecast in high school and probably are now at work. But whether you're the A Student, Underachiever, Geek, Activist, Complainer, or some combination of our two-dozen archetypes, it's not too late to reinvent or reinvigorate yourself. Our goal is to help you downplay the traits that hurt you, pump up the skills that help you, and "round yourself out" by adopting the best traits from your class . . . er, workmates. Think of our book as the best friend who'll tell you honestly how you're coming across to others.

Here's how to use it.

Find yourself in the archetypes

The archetypes are sorted into two groups: those at the top of the class and those in the bottom.

The top of the class includes folks like the Thespian, Teacher's Pet, Jock, Cheerleader, Underachiever, and Party Animal. These likable folks come in all shapes, sizes, colors, and genders. Their values, looks, priorities, pleasures, and peccadilloes may be different, but one thing they all have in common is their fundamental decency. Most readers will find themselves in this section.

The troublemakers in the bottom of the class are a different story. The Gossip, Snob, Know-it-all, Cheater, Prima Donna, and other disagreeable types also come in all shapes, sizes, colors, and genders. The one thing they all have in common is their impact—which is, sadly, negative. Most readers will recognize someone they've worked with in this section. (None of *us* would ever behave this way!) Since the folks in the bottom of the class don't get exposed or punished nearly enough at work, as a service to our readers we made sure they did in our book.

Identify your type's core communication strengths
Each archetype's description includes a list of the type's core communication strengths. Our aim is to help you leverage your best traits for maximum success and influence in the workplace.

Identify your type's core communication weaknesses
Each archetype's description includes a list of the type's core weaknesses. Our aim here is to help you prevent them from sabotaging your credibility and undermining your success.

Blend
We said you were typecast in high school and probably are at work, too. If you want to reinvent or reinvigorate your type, the solution is to blend. We encourage you to study all the types in the book and think about the traits you admire. When the charismatic Party Animal decides it's time to strengthen his credentials, he might look to the A Student or the Class President for guidance. The Rebel was recently promoted but knows she needs to be more of a team player, so she studies the Cheerleader, Party Animal, Jock, and others in the top of the class.

To illustrate blends, we've included examples.

- **Premium Blends** are best-case scenarios, achieved when positive archetypes from the top of the class are combined. These are examples only and are not meant to be prescriptive.
- **Poisonous Blends** are worst-case scenarios, achieved when negative archetypes from the bottom of the class are combined with other classmates. As there are no desirable blends that include a member of the bottom of the class, these are *definitely* not meant to be prescriptive.

You don't get a second chance at high school; but there's still plenty of time to improve your image and reputation at work, to make the most of your natural style, and to boost your chances for professional success. As the writer George Eliot said, "It's never too late to be what you might have been."

So, let's get started, class.

PART ONE

THE CLASS

True terror is to wake up one morning and discover that your high school class is running the country.

—KURT VONNEGUT

THE TOP OF THE CLASS

THE A STUDENT

It takes twenty years to become an overnight success.

—EDDIE CANTOR

Not only did A Students turn all assignments in on time, they *liked* doing homework. While the rest of us sighed in relief because we had actually passed the physics test with the nothing-to-be-proud-of-but-still-miraculous 75, A Students sulked having scored *only* a 96. Nobody asked these students to submit term papers in clear plastic folders with blue cover pages and fancy borders, but A Students always did. And the teacher affectionately affixed gold stars next to their names in the grade book.

But it is a myth that the A Student is a genius. Sure, every school had its occasional piano prodigy or MIT-bound chemistry wizard. Yet, in most cases, A Students got A's because they simply went the extra mile. They completed all their work *and* the extra-credit assignments, and never complained about them or when they were due. Cramming was never their style. They were more diligent, more disciplined, and more determined. And they had a seemingly bottomless capacity to get work done, often with little instruction or oversight.

In the work world, most people who get promoted behave like A Students, even if they weren't the first time around. The secret to their success? They surpass the boss's expectations.

It's not hard to picture the A Student receiving the workplace equivalent of her report card: the annual performance appraisal. The boss opens the door to an excited, if slightly nervous, employee. The A Student knows she's completed all project assignments on time and has exceeded expectations, so she sits down, folds her hands, and waits for the accolades. And they come. A Students are lauded as role models. The boss is glowing about her "customer focus," "results orientation," "professionalism," and "expertise." A Students are a pleasure to work with and they inspire confidence in the department. The boss admits struggling to come up with *any* developmental advice for this employee. Perhaps, says the boss, the A Student might look for ways to strengthen memo-writing skills, which, overall, are already quite good.

Wow! What an evaluation! Most of us would do back-flips for an assessment that strong. But just a moment. Let's check in and see how our A Student is reacting. She's back at her desk pouring over a memo written earlier that day, looking for additional ways to revise and perfect it. And there's one other thing you can be certain of: before the A Student leaves the office she'll order copies of the latest books on business writing from an on-line bookseller. When they arrive, you can bet she'll read them diligently. Because an A without the gold star just isn't good enough. The A Student is already preparing for her next performance appraisal.

The A Student's Communication Style

- Their primary source of power is mental discipline: when around A Students, we can actually *feel* their seriousness of purpose. They communicate earnestness and focus. They are renowned for a strong sense of stick-to-it-ive-ness and work ethic.
- A Students frequently communicate their intensity, their drive to accomplish, in their body language and their voice. They gesture frequently, their eyes focus intently, and their voice is deliberate yet energetic.
- Because they listen well, A Students often ask valuable, clear, and direct questions to ensure they understand.
- Although A Students are very attuned to substance, they are also in the know about style and wardrobe. They package themselves well.

The A Student's Strengths

- *Preparation, preparation, preparation.* They are the ones at the meeting who prepared their key points in advance, wrote a summary for the boss to offer as a leave-behind, and brought stacks of backup data to support all claims.
- *Ability to listen and repeat.* Top students often record every word of a teacher's lecture, then hand the material right back to the teacher a week later in a different form, whether it's a term paper, pop quiz, or classroom discussion. Reviewing the term paper, the teacher is dazzled by the student's brilliant analysis and penetrating insights. "The kid really gets it!" the teacher says, then

smiles and scrawls A+ at the top of the report. It's exactly the same in the workplace. A Students like pleasing authority and getting it right.

- *Speed.* In high school, A Students' hands were always the first in the air when the teacher asked a question. The workplace is more subtle, but A Students enjoy the same natural advantage that comes with being better prepared than their colleagues. Thus, A Students jump into conversations quickly and gracefully. They identify and seize opportunities to piggyback off other people's comments. When others are speaking, A Students are flipping through their mind's files, looking for a fact to connect or insert into the conversation.

- *Leveraging credibility and control through language.* A Students use leading comments such as
  —"I looked into this issue before our meeting. Let me tell you what I learned. . . ."
  —"I hope you don't mind that I did more than you asked for. But once I dove into the assignment, I learned some things you'll find noteworthy."
  —"I'd like to follow up on something Susan just said. . . ."
  —"I want to make sure I understand the assignment correctly. You're asking me to. . . ."

What Undermines the A Student's Success

- *Inflexibility.* A Students are notorious control freaks. They didn't like it when the teacher put a question on the exam that was not addressed in the lecture or the readings. In high school, they could complain. In the workplace, they need to show they can improvise and go with the flow in an uncertain situation—even if it's uncomfortable.

- *Inability to separate the forest from the trees.* A Students often know more facts than anybody does. However, they must be careful not to get so bogged down in the facts that they forget the bigger picture—the broader ideas or themes they are discussing. They must remind themselves that spreadsheets and data, by themselves, do not add up to insight or analysis.

- *The know-it-all syndrome.* To be credible, A Students must explain ideas and information clearly, without patronizing or overusing detail. Knowledge alone won't move people to the top—they have to be likable as well. That takes attitude—the right attitude, that is.

- *Asking too many questions.* While A Students may ask relevant questions to ensure that they get all the details right, others may interpret their questions differently. In highly competitive environments, questions are sometimes seen as challenges to authority. And they can make colleagues impatient.

If Your Boss or Colleague is an A Student

- *Match or exceed expectations.* Pay careful attention to what they do and how they like things done. The best way to thrive under or with an A Student is to mirror their work ethic.

- *Accept the fact that A Student bosses will micromanage you.* They can't help it—it's part of their DNA. Just do the very

best work you can, smile, and say "No problem" when
the boss suggests that you use ivory paper and a green
binder for your report instead of the white paper and yel-
low binder that you've already printed and assembled.

- *Look for ways to complement their skills set.* If you are a
dazzling organizer of presentations, offer to help look
for slides that would best accompany your boss's or colleague's subject matter. Soon you may find yourself an
indispensable asset.

- *Be grateful.* If your boss is an A Student, you can be
pretty well assured that your department will be in ship
shape and that upper management will be pleased with
what they see. The better your department's reputation,
the more likely you are to be rewarded. And remember:
You have a terrific example to emulate whenever you
want to improve your overall work habits.

Premium Blends

- *The A Student–Thespian.* This type can be a workplace
powerhouse. Pure A Students are disciplined and con-
scientious, but are often so busy trying to give teachers
and bosses what they want that they can forget to express
themselves. The Thespian, on the other hand, is all about
self-expression. The classic salesperson, this type gives
you a dazzling presentation about whatever he's selling—
and can back it up with facts, figures, and statistics.

- *The A Student–Underachiever.* This combination may
seem like a contradiction, but don't be fooled. While
the Underachiever lacks the discipline of an A Student

(and often a B Student, for that matter), the Underachiever has an ability to improvise and produce work that comes right from the gut, sometimes stunning a boss or teacher. (Since most of the Underachiever's work is done at the last minute, how could he do anything but rely on gut instincts?) The A Student, on the other hand, has been thinking through the project so exhaustively that it's possible he has thought its original spark right out of it. The point is not to start your work the night before it's due but rather to allow yourself and your work a little spontaneity. The combination of these seemingly antithetical archetypes can produce great results.

- *The A Student–Cheerleader.* Not all A Students have a problem working in teams, but enough of them could take a lesson or two from the optimistic and supportive Cheerleader who values collaboration and teamwork. A Students typically want to stand apart from others and, as a result, tend to be naturally competitive, while the A Student–Cheerleader blend puts individual achievement aside, celebrating departmental and company pride instead. Additionally, the A Student–Cheerleader offers kind words of encouragement, helps bring out everyone's best work, and will never drop the ball on an assignment.

Poisonous Blend

- *The A Student–Prima Donna.* From the moment this perfection seeker with a rock star attitude comes into your department *at your very same job level,* the A Student– Prima Donna behaves as if you and everyone else exist to serve and ensure the Prima Donna's success. The only person who doesn't seem to notice is the boss, who praises the A Student–Prima Donna's work, somehow missing the fact that it takes a team effort to get the project finished. Grace is, unfortunately, what this blend lacks; and A Student–Prima Donnas will undoubtedly find themselves shaking their heads and wondering why nobody likes them.

THE CLASS CLOWN

Laughter is the shortest distance between two people.

—VICTOR BORGE

The Class Clown's impersonation of the school librarian, Mrs. Hardwig, had everyone laughing so hard at the lunch table that milk sprayed out of their nostrils. Later that day, in biology class, everyone was similarly entertained when he waved a scalpel and taunted a formaldehyde-scented dead frog with questions about its medical history. Even the teacher was laughing.

When they didn't go too far, Class Clowns attracted audiences and spotlights. They often deflected others' hard knocks with their softer jabs, smoothed out uncomfortable moments with their light touch, and turned attention toward themselves. High school was good training for the business world, where audiences and spotlights are sought-after prizes, and where laughter can lighten the mood at a contentious meeting or even seal a business deal.

In the workplace, the Class Clown's greatest skills include being able to disarm colleagues, defuse anger or skepticism, build camaraderie, and heighten morale. For example, the two rivals at the weekly staff meeting have been sparring for six months. During a particularly tense moment, the clown raises his hand and in a voice that is steady and slow asks if it might be possible to resolve this dispute as professional wrestlers would by installing a ten-foot-high steel cage in the conference room and having a Texas death match. As the laughter fades, so does the hostility.

Clowns can be just as effective on paper.

Let's look in on the Class Clown Human Resources VP, for example. The VP's staff has been pulling long hours to complete a compensation study needed for the company's board meeting next week. The staff has also been leaving messy leftover food trays all over the office, much to the dismay of the facilities manager.

What to do? If the VP issues an e-mail scolding the staff, the likely reaction will be resistance and lower morale. Instead, the wit of this Class Clown proved the perfect anecdote and antidote to rescue the situation through the following e-mail:

TO: A Hardworking and Hungry Staff   **DATE:** June 6
FROM: S. A. Davidson
SUBJECT: Uninvited Guests at Dinner

When I arrived at the office at 7:00 A.M., several uninvited revelers of the *Blattaria Cucaracha* family ("bugs" for short) greeted me, informing me how much they enjoyed the leftover food around the office. They even assured me they are going to tell all their friends where the best bites can be found. And they promised to return again to party.

So we've got a quick choice to make: we can return our trays to the cafeteria, as Jim Drake from Facilities has reminded us, or we can expect to share our space with more of these uninvited and unwelcome guests.

I realize you can surely use extra hands and heads as you work to complete our compensation report, but I doubt if these *Blattaria Cucaracha* are the heads and hands you had in mind.

Your efforts to make me look good at the board meeting are not unnoticed—I'll bring in today's pizza. And I promise to take out the garbage after.

Class clowns often see situations in a new light, and they offer a fresh perspective. They perform more than just capers. In their writing and in their conversation, they illustrate the power of the pen, er, pun and replace the terminal boredom of the workplace with wit and personality. At their best, they know how to blend good humor with a human touch. What's more, they make friends quickly and people generally like them—if they don't go too far.

The Class Clown's Communication Style

- Class Clowns draw their power from their speed and timing. Not only do they have a sense of *what* to say, they also know *when* to say it. This ability gives them command presence in any room.

- Their lack of self-consciousness about their bodies creates a physical presence, through uninhibited use of body language to emphasize their points.
- When talking, Class Clowns are clever. While most of us would be troubled at finding a coffee stain on our slacks right before a big presentation, Class Clowns aren't. Instead, they find a way to use the stain to their advantage—and often relax and win the audience over in the process. They do not embarrass easily, if at all.

The Class Clown's Strengths

- *Timing.* His most important skill is not a sense of humor but a sense of timing. Class Clowns always seem to know the right moment to break in with something funny.
- *Preparation and a good memory.* Oscar Wilde was known for making amazingly well-timed quips at dinner parties. "I can resist everything except temptation," he proclaimed as a decadent dessert was offered. What his dinner companions didn't know was that he'd conceived that line at breakfast. He simply waited for the perfect moment to trot it out. Class Clowns often "file away" funny thoughts, puns, and clever language and later insert them strategically into conversations, e-mails, and meetings, with great results.
- *Using humor to open doors.* A good opening line hooks the audience. Once they've got them hooked, Class Clowns don't let their audiences get away. They quickly transition into a conversation about business. Humor is

an effective tool but it is only a tool. It's a prop, not a crutch.

What Undermines the Class Clown's Success

- *Joking too much and working too little.* The Class Clown is more likely to get promoted for work product, judgment, loyalty, and reliability than for merely the ability to make people laugh. Whether accurate or not, the perception of Class Clowns is often that they don't focus enough on their work. Remember Proverbs: "Even a fool, when he holds his peace, is counted wise."

- *Confusing sarcasm with humor.* Clowns make fun of themselves and the world around them, and make a lot of friends in the process. The sarcastic make fun of others and turn people off. Class Clowns must remember to keep the humor positive and constructive.

- *Joking about the wrong topics.* Comments, however lighthearted, about race, ethnicity, gender, sexual orientation, politics, and religion should be avoided lest the Class Clown offend a colleague. When it comes to workplace humor, it's safest to err on the side of caution by not going too far. The Clown needs to remember to use common sense along with comic sense.

- *Appearing one-dimensional.* Class Clowns deserve to be taken seriously. Others in the workplace who see the Clown from a narrow-angled lens miss his more multidimensional splendor, where wit is only one facet of the Clown's ability. Ultimately, the Class Clown has to mirror the values of the organization.

If Your Boss or Colleague Is a Class Clown

- *Lighten up.* Let your boss or colleague know you are not without a humor-appreciation gene. Try understanding the circumstances and the purpose for the boss or colleague's humor. If it's well conceived, enjoy it and smile. It it's not, tactfully avoid becoming a part of it.
- *Exercise your own humor muscle.* Practice by sharing a humorous anecdote about yourself, your family, or a pet, choosing a lunchroom setting or coffee break rather than a more formal or disruptive moment. Spar back occasionally. You might even enjoy it!
- *Avoid being around a distasteful Class Clown.* It's easy to enjoy a good joke, but it's not so easy to stand by when the joke is over the line or insulting. If such is the case, quietly and quickly remove yourself from earshot.

Premium Blends

- *The Class Clown–Activist.* This blend has the power to get people to do things they otherwise might not normally do, to believe in causes they might not have thought of supporting, to diffuse the tension when the air is thickest. Whether it was Mark Twain a century ago or Bill Cosby today, it's a gifted sort who can make you laugh and think at the same time.
- *The Class Clown–Geek.* This type is delightfully weird. What fun it is to work with someone who can solve any problem, unravel any riddle, and keep you laughing at the same time.

- *The Class Clown–Jock.* Get ready for a double dose of charisma. In this blend you'll find the physical presence to command a room and be noticed and admired, and a personality that's likable and pleasant to be around.

Poisonous Blend

- *The Class Clown–Gossip.* This type tends to play too lightly with other people's feelings and reputations. It exhibits the traits that undermine the Class Clown's success, making malicious one-liners about all the wrong stuff. This type operates more successfully as a gossip columnist, or sparring on late-night television—or on a Las Vegas stage.

THE REBEL

Whoso would be a man must be a nonconformist.

—RALPH WALDO EMERSON

This student was way too cool for school. It wasn't hard to peg the Rebel: whatever the in-crowd was doing, the Rebel was doing the opposite. All the other students pined for a gleaming new car; the Rebel drove a cool vintage Dodge. The Rebel found the notion of being just like everyone else detestable, and went to great lengths to cultivate an image, a look, and a personality that was different from the pack's. The most interesting Rebel caused sensations and created trends—and abandoned them the instant others jumped on the bandwagon.

In the adult workplace, the Rebel's mantra is, "Why do it like everybody else?"

Unlike the rebel without a cause, who dropped out of high school in protest against the System, never to be heard from again, the Rebel within a workplace can be a constructive force for change. Take, for example, the Rebel advertising copywriter who says, "Why does every TV commercial for floor wax feature the same woman with a pearl necklace and blindingly white teeth dancing a ballet across the kitchen floor?"

"Because that's the way we've always done it," say the Rebel's colleagues. "We need to show the product in a favorable light." But the workplace Rebel isn't buying it. "Why don't we show what people *really* look like when they clean their houses on Saturday morning. We'll put them in sweats, hair tangled up, yelling at the kids."

Thirteen different people had to review and sign off on the idea, but the unconventional ad finally got made. The ad was a hit with consumers and the floor wax became the top seller in its category.

Indeed, the Rebel at work can be sophisticated and savvy in her rebellion, a trendsetter ahead of the conforming crowd. Many possess immense creativity and vision, even genius, seeing things the rest of us don't. Their memos and reports reflect how they differentiate themselves: they might not even bother to write the weekly report—or, if they choose to, they won't follow the required template.

The Rebel's Communication Style

- Whether on paper, over the phone, or in person, the Rebel looks and sounds different. Whatever the pack is doing, the Rebel communicates the opposite. Rebels become who they are by paying very close attention to what they *don't* want to become. If the work culture is formal, the Rebel writes, speaks, and presents informally. If the dress code is blue jeans and T-shirts, the Rebel dresses up. Unless Rebels model themselves after a 1950s cliché (the monosyllabic leather-jacketed motorcycle-riding thug), most workplace Rebels are good talkers, writers, and presenters, and they enjoy facility with language.

- Rebels provoke. They ask thoughtful questions and challenge their co-workers to see things differently.
- Rebels are precise communicators. Because they don't want to be lumped in with "average" people, they pay a lot of attention to detail and differentiation. As a result, their presentation of words, images, ideas, and themselves is fresh and attention getting.

The Rebel's Strengths

- *Keen observational skills.* Rebels often have tremendously good eyes, ears, and instincts. If their clothing style trends are two years ahead of everyone else's, so too are their opinions about industry trends or the potential popularity of a new product or way of doing business.
- *Compromise.* Huh? This seems counterintuitive, but it's true. Rebels who are inflexible and insufferable are also unemployable. Successful Rebels are skilled at being a little different but not *too* different. They provoke but never frighten. They're different but they don't alienate.
- *Creativity and imagination.* Rebels are Rebels because they are, well . . . *different.* By continuing to offer a fresh perspective, they get noticed and, if they can get along with others, get promoted.

- *Conviction.* Rebels rebel for a reason: the company is doing it the old way, the hard way, the dumb way; and they want to do it the new way, the better way, the smart way. They notice things first. They aren't just striking a pose; they really *are* different. If they can communicate their perspective constructively, with tact and passion, they can transform their companies.

What Undermines the Rebel's Success

- *Negative advertising.* Rebels have to be careful that they don't install a virtual neon sign over their heads that reads: "I'm smarter than you." "I'm cooler than you." "I'm more creative than you."
- *Challenging authority.* Four hundred years before Christ's birth, students of the great philosopher Socrates were encouraged to constantly challenge, question, cross-examine, and refute. This quest for truth and understanding, later known as the Socratic method, transformed learning, ideas, and civilization itself. Today, some Rebels confuse the modern workplace with ancient Greece. They do so at their peril: the Socratic method is not enthusiastically received at distribution centers, financial services firms, automotive-parts factories, high-rise office buildings, temp-service agencies, and other work venues. Rebels must remember that there is a difference between debating the existence of God and debating the Finance Department's policy of issuing paychecks on the first and fifteenth days of the month.

- *Rebellion for rebellion's sake.* The Rebel can seem juvenile. The server at the restaurant knows dangling earrings are prohibited, but wears them anyway as a badge of independence or protest. Wearing leather pants to the accounting firm will shock, and does; the Rebel gets points for nerve. But once the shock wears off, colleagues, clients, and bosses are annoyed, not intrigued or impressed. Even worse are the Rebels who think that tattooing curse words or offensive images on their necks or arms makes them Rebels. It does not; it makes them idiots. An adult Rebel rebels with the mind, not the body.

If Your Boss or Colleague Is a Rebel

- *Declare your independence.* Better yet, *show* it, don't just say it. The Rebel prizes nonconformity and individuality. The Rebel will be one of the few people you'll ever report to or work with who is thrilled you don't want to look, talk, act, and dress like everyone else. Take advantage of this rare opportunity.
- *Keep changing.* Rebels like phrases like "new and improved" a lot more than "the same since 1882." They are constantly reinventing themselves. Try not to become too predictable. This doesn't mean you have to dye your hair purple. It simply means being mindful of not thinking or saying things the same way over and over again.
- *Keep your rules and regulations to yourself.* Rebels hate personnel manuals, policy memos, and any form of bu-

reaucracy. If you like rules and live to be governed by them, that's okay. But reminding your Rebel boss or colleague what it says in section 34B, paragraph 7 of the employees' manual about bringing houseplants to work will not endear you.

Premium Blends

- *The Rebel–Straight Arrow.* A formidable mix, this type seeks to blend in. Bosses and colleagues are often threatened by the too independent or too rebellious. The Rebel's rough edges are softened when mixed with the Straight Arrow's attributes like loyalty. This type is often very politically astute, a revolutionary in a Brooks Brothers suit with the patience to change the world one day at a time.
- *The Rebel–Class Clown.* The workers in the shipping department hated change, and refused to change, until the Rebel–Class Clown supervisor showed up. Disarmed by the supervisor's wit and dared to innovate, the workers improved productivity by thirty percent. This type is particularly good at "wrapping the pill in chocolate"— that is, at persuading people and organizations to swallow medicine then being thanked for administering the dose.
- *The Rebel–Go-getter.* Herein lies a potent mixture of independence and courage. Utterly fearless, this type, whether a clerk in the mail room or a senior executive, tells the CEO morale stinks and there are five things that need to be done immediately if she expects to avoid a

mass employee exodus. The Rebel–Go-getter will either be fired or become the CEO's top adviser.

Poisonous Blend

- *The Rebel–Snob.* Nonconformists can be not only off-putting but also threatening to co-workers and bosses. They must be careful not to scare people. When the nonconformist adopts an attitude, he or she will be perceived as haughty, arrogant, and aloof, and will find few allies or champions in the workplace.

THE JOCK

Individual commitment to a group effort—that is what makes a team work, a company work, a society work, a civilization work.

—VINCE LOMBARDI

In high school, Jocks moved through the hallways like jungle cats, a mixture of muscle and grace, while the rest of us slouched, fidgeted, and fretted over our awkward teenage physiques. Rare at any age, but especially at seventeen, these lucky souls were in total command of their bodies. We knew it and they knew it. Whether the Jock was college scholarship material or a third-string bench-warmer wasn't really the point. With their enviable physical prowess, Jocks dripped confidence and charisma. They had *presence.* They won the most coveted prizes that high school awards its winners: lots of attention. On and off the field.

A little older, the workplace Jock still struts a peacock's tail. Sure, today everything's slightly more saggy, but the Jock still has physical presence. While more at ease reading about sports than torts, Jocks at work are still at the top of their game. And the Jock's charisma is as fit as ever.

It doesn't have to be the supersized college ring that first iden-
tifies the Jock at a staff meeting, although that and the Jock's physical presence *are* top indicators. Endorphins and energy are plentiful
in the Jock's bloodstream. Just watch him at that meeting. Working
the room, smiling, laughing, and telling stories. The Jock is in constant motion, angling the body, twisting, or slapping a colleague's
shoulder. Jocks have a hard time sitting still.

What's more, you'll hear Jocks, years after their championship
seasons are over, still "toughening up" one another for the rigors
of the game—this time, the game of business. They do it by nee-
dling, sparring, and challenging one another in a style reminiscent
of their locker-room towel snapping back in high school. Long
after their athletic careers are over, the Jocks' competitive spirit is
alive and well.

You can see other signs around the workplace, too. Jocks have
a regimen for exercise that distinguishes them from us weekend
walkers. You'll see them running off to the gym at lunchtime or
after the day's events, getting in their exercise. And if they're road
warriors as well, you can be sure they book themselves into hotels
with health clubs in-house or nearby. The Jock successfully balances
work and play.

The Jock's Communication Style

- The Jock's primary source of power is physical comportment. Jocks usually create a presence easily, through
  their physical size and fitness level. They literally muscle
  their way in to conversations and situations.
- Jocks walk tall. They have a confident stride that says "I
  can do the job."

- When speaking, the Jock is informal and comfortable. Naturally, the Jock favors sports analogies along the lines of "a full-court press," "it was a slam dunk," and "we hit a home run with that one."
- The Jock is sociable and talkative, with a relaxed speech pattern. Many Jocks use lazy language, forgetting to put endings on words and slurring words together. For example, the Jock may say "gonna" for "going," "doin' " for "doing," and "howzitgoin'?" for "how is it going?"
- The Jock has replaced the varsity uniform with other branded clothing that continues to reinforce membership on "the team" and that shows off a fit figure.

The Jock's Strengths

- *Physical presence.* Jocks are often blessed with good looks and a nice physique, and they put both to work. At their best, they let their physical presence make a confident but not cocky statement about themselves.
- *Winning business friends and influencing people.* In the workplace, the Jock's congeniality and confidence make him a natural leader. Jocks get along with everybody. Ever wonder where the term "team player" comes from?
- *Taking advantage of sports skill.* The Jock has learned that playing golf, tennis, squash, softball, or simply jogging with people from work can do as much for career advancement as a well-crafted memo or report.

What Undermines the Jock's Success

- *Displaying too much brawn and not enough brain.* Unfortunately, the "dumb jock" stereotype haunts some people in adulthood. But Jocks who polish their language skills, speak clearly, slowly, and forcefully, and talk enthusiastically about subjects besides sports can turn this stereotype on its head.
- *Showboating.* High school coaches bench players who hog the spotlight and forget they're part of a team. In high school and in the workplace, the coach/boss has more authority than the player does. Jocks must always remember this and show due respect.
- *Turning the body into a liability rather than an asset.* The Jock's physical presence can sometimes intimidate others. Colleagues would prefer to view them as gentle giants rather than King Kong. Likewise, while it's comfortable and natural for Jocks to be physical with others, physical contact of any kind in the workplace can be hazardous and is best avoided.
- *Not exercising the ears.* Because they are such good talkers, and because of their competitive instincts, Jocks may not take time to listen. Those who become good listeners will find that people around them appreciate the opportunity to be heard.

If Your Boss or Colleague Is a Jock

- *Read the sports page along with the business section.* You'll impress your Jock boss or colleague in a positive way by knowing what's going on with their favorite teams. A few brownie points can't hurt. In addition, if you have a favorite team that opposes your boss or colleague's, don't worry about some friendly competition. Good Jocks thrive on it.

- *Use sports analogies.* Jocks like having a language of their own. They prefer understanding business concepts in the terms of their sport. Let them know you're also in the game. Take a swing. Wrestle the issues to the ground. Go for the touchdown. Take the competition to the mat. Get to the finish line first. Don't wipe out.
- *Let the Jock reminisce.* Judiciously. That is, remember there's a difference between flattery and sincerity. Ask Jocks about their glory days when the time's appropriate—at lunch, while on a business trip together, winding down after a long day. It's a way of showing interest in his life, of seeing the bigger picture, of validating his way of seeing the world.

Premium Blends

- *The Jock–Class President.* Combine charisma with stamina and the ability to get along with a lot of people, and you've got the stuff of United States presidents. President Gerald Ford was president of his class, captain of the Michigan football team, and later, healer of a nation.
- *The Jock–Go-getter.* Stamina and courage are two of the key attributes of someone who is successful in sales or as an entrepreneur. Not surprisingly, lots of ex-athletes excel in both fields.

- *The Jock–Thespian.* Think of this type as the linebacker who goes to ballet school. This magnetic, high-energy type is in as much command of his voice and personality as he is in command of his body.

Poisonous Blend

- *The Jock–Bully.* Watch out! This type strikes a commanding pose in the workplace verbally and physically. Think intimidation with a capital *I*. This combination of archetypes may have worked in the past to organize a union or to propel a company turnaround. Such a style works only for the short term, where toughness and edge may be needed. But not for the long haul.

THE TEACHER'S PET

Faultless to a fault.

—ROBERT BROWNING

The hand shot up in the air.

"I believe the answer is Angola, Mr. Reynolds."

"That's absolutely right," replied the teacher with a smile. With that, the Teacher's Pet sat ramrod straight, hands folded, eyes fixed forward on the teacher, who wrote the answer on the board and underlined it twice: Angola. The bell rang. Sophomores scurried.

"Can you stick around a minute?" asked the teacher of the Pet. When the classroom was empty, the student approached the teacher's desk.

"What's up, Mr. R.?"

"Let me tell you something. You're a real wiz at geography."

The Teacher's Pet shrugged and smiled, glowing inwardly.

"I have another student struggling with this material. How would you feel about lending a hand? Maybe spend some time going over the maps and so on," said the teacher.

"I'd be happy to tutor anyone else who's having a hard time, if it'll help you out, Mr. R. See, geography's kind of my hobby."

This was the beginning of a beautiful friendship.

We've all had teachers we admired, even adored, and that unconditional love showed itself in many ways: our classroom volunteerism, our protection of that teacher's reputation in the presence of those less infatuated, and our planned loitering near the classroom door. The admiration society was mutual and, most important, real. We shared the teacher's passion about the subject taught, and our personalities clicked.

Now fast-forward to the office.

The Prince of Darkness (a.k.a. Dale from Purchasing) is coming down the hall.

The Teacher's Pet intercepts Dale.

"Dale! Hello! What brings you over our way? Pat is going to be so sorry to have missed you. Anything I can help you with?"

The Teacher's Pet stands tall in front of the boss's door. Dale's not getting in that door. No way.

"You saved my life!" says Pat to the Pet, fifteen minutes later.

Yes, the boss can always count on the Teacher's Pet's unrelenting protection twenty-four seven, if need be. Indeed, loyalty, reliability, and respect are highly regarded traits at any age, and in any place—the classroom or the workplace. After all, who wouldn't mind a loyal follower, a faithful sidekick, someone offering unconditional love in the dog-eat-dog world of business?

And though we may find ourselves talking about the Teacher's Pet at the water cooler occasionally, we know why. Admit it, we're actually a little envious. We'd all like that kind of access to those with power.

The Teacher's Pet's Communication Style

- Teacher's Pets draw their power from the ability to connect with their "sponsors." The communications between the Teacher's Pet and the sponsor can be almost like a married couple's, where one partner starts a sentence and the other finishes it.
- Her language will often echo the boss's, right down to specific words. Favorite expressions and phrases of the boss's will be captured and work their way verbatim into the memos written or directives offered to others. In other words, the Teacher's Pet is usually an excellent summarizer, remembering and repeating the boss's key themes and ideas.
- When in the boss's presence, the Teacher's Pet's body language will show not merely respect but awe. The eyes will mirror attentiveness; the body will also be at attention, maybe even a bit stiff.
- The Teacher's Pet is sincere when replying "Yes," "No problem," and "Right away" to the boss's requests.
- The Teacher's Pet is a gifted listener. She hears everything, files it away, and plays it back later. For example, the Teacher's Pet will buy Stevie Wonder's greatest hits as a present for the boss, who was humming along with "Isn't She Lovely" on the car radio when the two of them were on the way to the airport.

The Teacher's Pet's Strengths

- *Expertise.* Anyone can suck up and get the boss coffee—
  and some Teacher's Pets do. But the savvy Teacher's Pet
  is the one who read the newspaper and saw an article
  that the boss should read. Teacher's Pets readily establish
  that they are great friends to the boss. But they become
  vital assets, too. They stay on top of the issues, knowing
  that keeping up will keep them at their boss's side.
- *Perspective.* More than tacit agreement, the boss needs to
  look at all angles and repercussions possible from the
  decisions made. Talented Teacher's Pets do more than
  merely agree; they serve as the devil's advocate from
  time to time. Of course, they do so tactfully. Instead of
  telling the boss, "That's a stupid idea," they say, "Have
  you thought about . . ." or "Another way to look at it
  might be. . . ."
- *Independence.* Talented Teacher's Pets don't let their identity get swallowed up by the boss. While they may echo
  the opinions and language of those in power, they also
  stretch. They cultivate the ability to see things through
  their own well-focused lens. Sometimes that picture will
  mirror the views held by the boss, sometimes not. Successful Teacher's Pets dare to be their own people. The
  most successful are the ones who enjoy special access to
  power and leverage it for long-term career success.
- *Follow-through.* When they say you'll have the figures on
  your desk by 3:00 P.M., Teacher's Pets mean it. They
  never miss deadlines and always keep their word. This

reliability makes them the perfect "go to" person for the boss.

What Undermines the Teacher's Pet's Success

- *Stepping on others.* While it's comfortable to be in the boss's inner circle, the Teacher's Pet can easily become a target to those who are not. If she's too busy doing the boss's bidding, the Teacher's Pet may become blinded by the "light from above" and thus forget about colleagues who can subvert her efforts. In other words, the Teacher's Pet must remember to treat others the way she treats the boss—with respect.

- *Being mislabeled a Brown-noser.* Being a faithful sidekick, always ready to do the boss's bidding, the Teacher's Pet can make colleagues uneasy or even jealous. The smart Teacher's Pet realizes some are going to talk behind her back. She will have to expect, ignore—and handle—the behind-the-scenes name-calling.

- *Putting all the eggs in one basket.* The Teacher's Pet needs to remember that the boss might not always be in power. While it does feel good to be associated with someone who's at the top, in today's job market, that power is potentially short-lived. Thus, Teacher's Pets need to develop their own set of credentials, so that when the boss moves on, the Pet will still have a valuable role.

If Your Boss or Colleague Is a Teacher's Pet

- *Learn from them.* If your boss is a Teacher's Pet, observe how she responds to those up the command post so that you can learn what sells. After all, your job is to make your bosses look good, whose job, in turn, is to make their bosses look good. As long as you hold on to your own identity as well, it can't hurt to slip into the Teacher's Pet's skin to understand what it's like—and where it may get you.

- *Reserve jealousy.* If a colleague holds that special Teacher's Pet position with your boss, cool the complaining and work instead on developing your own skills. It also won't hurt to foster camaraderie with your colleague. Who knows, the Teacher's Pet just may need your help one day.

- *Find opportunities to be noticed.* Do good work. Volunteer to be on project teams. Since the Teacher's Pet is the "go-to" person for the boss, let the Teacher's Pet realize you can be counted on as well. This trickle-down reliability can work in your favor.

Premium Blends

- *Teacher's Pet–Straight Arrow.* When the strengths of the Teacher's Pet—reliability, perspective, and expertise—are combined with the capability, integrity, and authenticity of the Straight Arrow, their bosses can't help but make smarter decisions. Bosses often find themselves in danger when they surround themselves with only yes-men and yes-women, the Brown-nosers who dare not disagree. But when they ask for recommendations from the Teacher's Pet–Straight Arrow, bosses will hear the truth, whether they like it or not. This reliable type will remind the boss of important details she might have overlooked. And that truth can preserve not only the company's bottom line but its reputation as well.

- *Teacher's Pet–Cheerleader.* Who better to make bosses or colleagues feel up when business is down, energized when exhausted, and able to lean back without falling down?

Poisonous Blend

- *The Teacher's Pet–Bully.* Is there a nightmare worse than someone who has special access to the boss and on top of that spends her free time terrorizing you? This is when faithful sidekicks like the Lone Ranger's Tonto or Batman's Robin get fused with one of the thugs from *Goodfellas* in a terrible science experiment gone wrong. Steer clear!

THE GEEK

Uncool people never hurt anybody—all they do is collect stamps, read science-fiction books and stand on the end of railway platforms staring at trains.

—BEN ELTON, *RADIO TIMES*

At fourteen, Geeks had already figured out how to run electricity through their braces. While classmates were leering at the swimsuit edition of *Sports Illustrated* or reading *Cosmo* for the latest diet and fashion fads, the Geek fantasized about becoming MIT "cubed"—earning a bachelor's, master's, and doctoral degree in quantum physics. The Geek was reserved and humble, with lots of intellectual muscle.

While others wondered if their Saturday night party plans would materialize, Geeks knew theirs with certainty: lost episodes of *Star Trek* would entertain only after reading the latest issues of *Computer Age* and college catalogues. Throughout the ages, the Geek has relied on instruments: slide rules in the '50s, calculators in the '70s, Palm Pilots, pagers, and laptop computers in the '90s, and all things wireless into the twenty-first century. For the Geek the right answers were readily computed in solid geometry, but less attainable in social situations.

So it is in the workplace. The Geek tends to be a quiet contributor, less involved and interested in office politics, and usually not in anyone's way. Leading from the brain, the Geek is often more interested in concepts than conversation. Imagine your coworkers Rob and Nikki chatting in the copier room, discussing the latest office romances as they wait for the copier to collate 750 copies of the latest office policies manual. Enter the Geek, on a mission to make copies of a just-finished productivity analysis. Seeing the copier in use and with no aspirations to join in Rob and Nikki's chitchat, the Geek returns to the office and begins to outline recommendations for next week's strategy session. Indeed, the Geek is about substance, *not* sizzle.

The Geek's Communication Style

- Expertise, more than personality, fuels the Geek's confidence and communication style.
- Geeks are often fountains of ideas and information, but need help turning on the spigot.
- When explaining information to others, the Geek tends to be slow, methodical, dry, and technical.
- Some Geeks speak only when asked to. Small talk is rare—and awkward.
- The Geek relies on the facts to communicate his message. A favorite phrase is "According to the research . . ."
- Whether in dress, physical comportment, or soft-spoken communication style, the Geek often stands apart from the crowd.

The Geek's Strengths

- *"Getting it" when others don't.* Geeks have enviable IQs and an amazing capacity to understand highly technical, complicated material that too easily frustrates or bores others. Quite simply, Geeks are *smart*.
- *Depth of focus and attention to detail.* Geeks slice deeply into the "why" of things, often with a patience unknown to most. They wage war with ambiguity, always seeking answers, and are usually victorious.
- *Thinking both inside and outside the box.* Geeks find new ways of solving problems or variations of old ways to produce better results. They are the architects of tunnels and inventors of vaccines; they are the men and women who have taken us from the TV full of tubes to the flat plasma screen; from the first flight in North Carolina to the moon; and from darkness to the lightbulb.

What Undermines the Geek's Success

- *Lack of plain talk.* Geeks understand their own language perfectly, but they must also translate their technical jargon into plain English for varied audiences. Geeks have a gift: They understand complex technical information. But true intelligence is multifaceted and Geeks need to be capable of helping others understand, too. When Geeks speak and write, they need to challenge themselves to eliminate jargon and communicate in clear, simple language. Plain-speaking technocrats soar. Once mastered, these skills will keep the Geek from being excluded—both in the lunchroom and the boardroom. Thus they can convey their ideas to others who are less technologically adept.

- *Timidity.* A Geek's high intelligence can shape a department or organization's direction, but only if he asserts himself. A Geek's innate quietness, soft-spokenness, and studious nature may be mistaken for fearfulness or aloofness. Geeks need to explain their ideas with brevity, clarity, and confidence—and not keep these to themselves.

- *Not blending in.* Geeks risk being shunned because others may feel inferior intellectually or superior socially, or both. Becoming more rounded will let others see them as more dimensional. Geeks are often exiled to the far corners of the office. It pays off when they take note of the corporate culture around them—for example, by noticing how others dress—and assimilate.

- *Paralysis of analysis syndrome.* While it's essential to get it right, many Geeks have trouble knowing when to stop designing and start executing their ideas. They delay action, not getting their ideas from the drawing board to the boardroom to the buyer in a timely fashion.

- *Not connecting with the audience.* Geeks tend to bore rather than dazzle their audiences when they explain technical issues. The more detail and jargon they use, the more likely the audience will get confused or sleepy. Geeks need to say it quickly and simply, and leave the audience hungry for more.

If Your Boss or Colleague Is a Geek

- *Encourage the Geek to be proactive versus reactive.* Because Geeks love analysis, they can get stuck in it and bog the department down by studying a situation too much or too long. Of course, quality is important, but in business, timing can be the villain or the hero of an idea. So whether the Geek is your boss or your colleague, you might need to gently push him toward action before it's too late.

- *Offer to serve as spokesperson/translator.* Geeks have a language of their own, and they often lack a sense of their audience. You can help the Geek boss or colleague be understood, sell an idea or a product in meetings and conferences, if you can relate well to the Geek and his audiences. Your ability to explain his complex ideas to others will turn you into an invaluable asset to both the Geek and the company.

- *Learn from the Geek.* What an opportunity to expand your knowledge base. Spend time trying to understand the Geek's intensity and intellect. Some of it may rub off on you.

Premium Blends

- *The Geek–Thespian.* In contrast to the Geek's natural quietness or shyness, the Geek–Thespian can be a strong presence at work, especially when giving a presentation in a meeting or at a conference. Idiosyncrasies and quirky interests are often reflected in their presentation style. This is the speaker who activates a strobe light or shows a *Star Trek* clip to illustrate an idea for the audience to grasp and grab. Most presenters would lack the nerve to try this, or get laughed off the stage. The Geek–Thespian pulls it off.

- *The Geek–A Student.* This morph can be dynamite in fields requiring quick action and decision making. Both have intensity and smarts, but the A Student has an added sense of timing and can work to meet deadlines more efficiently.

Poisonous Blend

- *The Geek–Know-it-all.* At its best, this combination irritates. At its worst, it can scare the dickens out of you. This blend has the brains to devise the weapon and the plan, and the attitude to move forward with a menacing certainty.

THE PARTY ANIMAL

Seven years of college down the drain!

—JOHN BELUSHI AS BROTHER BLUTO IN

ANIMAL HOUSE

Always up for a good time, the Party Animal knew exactly when someone's parents were going to be out of town for the weekend; he had the invites and directions to the party out well in advance. Yes, the Party Animal knew how to sniff and seek where the good times were. Party Animals even managed to go out on school nights, a feat rarely achieved by the rest of us. And it was a mortal sin for the Party Animal to spend Friday or Saturday night alone at home watching TV. Party Animals crave being with others.

Party Animals are no couch potatoes. They'll party alone, if they have to. In the workplace, they arrange the TGIF get-togethers each week after work, the birthday and anniversary surprises, and the department's summer outings. Party Animals like people and parties, and they'll find any excuse to celebrate. Just look at the Party Animal who has just turned a two-day management training session into a two-day rave.

After the all-day out-of-town sales meeting, our Party Animal told everyone to meet in the hotel lobby. Be assured, he has arranged to have the hotel van drive everyone to the best seafood restaurant in town; and afterward, they will all cab it to the town's hot spots. At 1:00 A.M. the next morning he will organize a Ping-Pong championship by the hotel pool that will keep everyone's adrenaline pumping into the wee hours.

"Oh, you've got to be kidding—you're not joining us?" you can expect the Party Animal to counter when you announce that you are exhausted and plan on going back to your room and ordering room service, rather than touring the sites or joining the beach party he's arranged. The Party Animal, looking at you in disbelief, asks, "What, are you nuts?!"

You see, Party Animals believe in the moment: they do not defer the opportunity for pleasure. "Carpe diem" is their mantra and they cannot fathom anyone *not* wanting to party. So if you're going to be working around Party Animals—or if you work *for* one—you'd better have a really good excuse for not joining the festivities.

Expect the Party Animal and his entourage to arrive the morning after with aspirin bottles in hand. Yet hangover and all, he miraculously makes it through a second day of meetings full of performance diagrams, sales figures, and good ideas. Non-Party Animals can't help but admire how these individuals manage to function. In enviable ways, they seem to grab the world by its tail and make the most of every moment.

The Party Animal's Communication Style

- Party Animals are born talkers. They love being around others and kibitzing. It matters little whether they are surrounded by strangers or friends. Their primary source of power comes from their affable nature and verbal skills.
- Party Animals are generally uninhibited in their speech, clothing, and mannerisms. They come across as relaxed about themselves and comfortable in just about any situation. In fact, they often like, and seek, attention at gatherings.
- Party Animals have outgoing personalities and make friends easily. They are lighthearted in demeanor and attitude. They take pressure at work in easy stride, and they help others de-stress as well.

The Party Animal's Strengths

- *Storytelling.* Party Animals can spin a yarn, put you on the edge of your seat, and hold your attention.
- *Friendly and optimistic nature.* Party Animals are social beings. They love being around people, make friends fast and easily, and value time spent with others. They will readily do a favor for a friend.
- *Persuasiveness.* Party Animals connect well with others and usually do well in sales positions. They find it natural and fun to sell others on their ideas, plans, and products.

What Undermines the Party Animal's Success

- *Talking more than listening.* The Party Animal enjoys being the life of the party, the center of attention; as a result, this bon vivant may not listen well to others. In the workplace, this behavior can cost sales, bonuses, or promotions.
- *Overloading with endless talk.* Party Animals tend to want the party to continue into the early hours of the morning, believing that everyone wants to hear just one more tale. Knowing when to fold is a key lesson for Party Animals to master. In sales, it means knowing when to close.
- *Behaving like a lightweight.* All play and no work will make Jack and Jill be taken less seriously at the office. Striking a balance between the seriousness and the sociableness of the workplace will take the Party Animal far.

If Your Boss or Colleague Is a Party Animal

- *Join the party.* Especially if the Party Animal is your boss. If you segregate yourself, you risk being dubbed a loner or kill joy, *not* a team player.
- *Be the designated driver.* If your nature is more reserved and your need to party less strong, you can offer to drive. You can keep the real Party Animals safe.
- *Remember what Mother always said.* Play nice. Join in. Have fun. But do so in moderation.

Premium Blends

- *Party Animal–Go-getter.* In this blend, sociability and ambition meet. Entertaining customers and clients is as natural as breathing to this type. No one seems to notice that between all the laughs, steaks, and bottles of wine the Party Animal–Go Getter is moving in to close the deal.
- *Party Animal–Straight Arrow.* The warmth and friendship of the Party Animal mixed with the loyalty and reliability of the Straight Arrow is a good match. This blend enjoys a good time, makes sure work isn't ignored, and keeps an eye on colleagues who are partying hard.
- *Party Animal–Class Clown.* The person who organizes the party and is also the life of it. The perfect master of ceremonies at conventions, meetings, and retirement roasts. Caution: When this type crosses the line, the results can be distasteful and embarrassing—a party gone way out of hand.

Poisonous Blend

- *Party Animal–Gossip.* This good-hearted, fun-loving colleague buys you another beer, coaxes you into telling your secrets, and then tells everyone else.

THE LONER

"Don't you want to join us?" I was recently asked by an acquaintance when he ran across me alone after midnight in a coffeehouse that was already almost deserted. *"No, I don't,"* I said.

—FRANZ KAFKA, *THE DIARIES*

Loners spent their time, well, alone. In high school, the Loner felt most comfortable not at school but at home in the bedroom—in the cave. In that safe place the Loner was free to dream and wonder. In their youth, Loners tried on the equivalent of dozens of costumes, always in search of the perfect style and fit. Occasionally they hung out with other loners, sharing little in common except outsider status. They didn't join clubs or sports teams because they would have been forced to interact with students who seemed to fit so neatly into their respective niches. The Loner is the ultimate introvert.

The workplace Loner also operates on the margins. Neither too visible nor too loud, Loners stay below the radar. They naturally gravitate toward work that does not require a high degree of communications acumen. At the grocery store, the Loner would rather endure teeth-chattering cold restocking the dairy cooler than have to chat with customers at the checkout counter. At corporate headquarters, the Loner would rather file than work in sales or service, would rather work in an R&D lab than in marketing.

Day after day, the Loner engages in very little conversation or emotional engagement with co-workers. He certainly won't ask personal questions like "So how was your weekend?" Throughout the course of the day, he will devise ingenious ways to avoid contact. The Loner's office may be next to a co-worker's, yet he will volley a dozen voice-mail messages back and forth rather than discuss an issue face-to-face. Instead of dropping by to discuss a pending project, he will write up a detailed memo, leaving it on a colleague's chair at lunchtime. And while lunchtime is ordinarily a chance for colleagues to socialize, the Loner eats alone, or walks alone, or sits on a bench alone and reads a book or magazine. Whether the Loner works in an office, a cubicle, or on a factory line, it's as though this type is coated in clear polyurethane: sealed off, impenetrable.

Just because Loners don't like to chat or bask in the limelight doesn't mean they don't like to work. Give them a task and watch them go to it. The Loner law clerk will spend hours researching and writing a detailed and eloquent brief for the firm's lead attorney. The Loner truck driver, alone mile after mile, gets the goods to their destination with reliable consistency. The Loner scientist methodically documents each stage of a long-term study that holds promise to cure multiple sclerosis.

The silence of the Loner is by no means empty; it is simply his preferred mode. And often, remarkable results come from it.

The Loner's Communication Style

- The Loner does not draw communications power from traditional sources such as title or position, prestige, or vocal energy.
- Most communication is low-key, understated. (The loud Loner is an oxymoron.)
- Spoken and physical communication is even, almost flat. Many Loners are effective writers, because writing offers a safe harbor for them to express themselves. Like the fictional Cyrano de Bergerac who, feeling no one could love him because of his gigantic nose, agreed to write incredible love letters for a friend to the woman they both loved, Loners can be persuasive—and even elegant—on paper.
- Posture and physical comportment may be slouched, withdrawn, or timid. Similarly, the Loner's wardrobe is not flashy and may be monochromatic. Their physical manner supports their standing apart rather than joining in.

The Loner's Strengths

- *Concentration.* Loners demonstrate an intense level of concentration for things that interest them. When Loners find work they enjoy, they can dazzle, even blow people away with their work.
- *Imagination.* Loners are often highly imaginative and contemplative human beings. Thinking outside the box

isn't a stretch for them since they live outside the box already. A Loner can be a sought-after idea person.

- *Introspection.* Indeed, the Loner's introspection offers great opportunity for thinking, watching, and recording.

What Undermines the Loner's Success

- *Estrangement.* Loners avoid people. This can be a problem in the workplace for a number of reasons, the main one being that a lot of opportunities to communicate ideas are missed. The Loner's evasive behavior can slow his career development, since promotions usually go to people who are comfortable interacting with others and who (to an appropriate degree) advertise their skills and successes. Developing public speaking and other communications skills can help improve the Loner's chances for success in the workplace.

- *Passivity.* Since the Loner doesn't want to engage in friendly water-cooler chat, imagine the steps taken to avoid conflict. Bullies and others from the bottom of the class happily exploit the Loner's desire to hide under a rock when people-problems occur. Daunting as the task seems, Loners must harness and apply their formidable imagination, concentration, and integrity to defend themselves when threatened. Clint Eastwood's characters may be men of few words, but the bad guys know not to mess with them.

- *Negative vibes.* Because Loners do not communicate energy and engagement, they are often perceived as listless or lethargic. They often find themselves being 'talked to' by supervisors about negative attitude. As difficult or unnatural as it may seem, a smile and a bit of enthusiasm—genuine or feigned—goes a long way in the workplace.

If Your Boss or Colleague Is a Loner

- *Respect his space*. Loners like their space, so don't impose on it more often than you need to. If the Loner is your boss, touch base but don't make a nuisance of yourself or take too long in his office when making your point.
- *Test the boundaries*. Engage the Loner in conversation. Invite him to join you and others for lunch. Stop by his desk and greet him when you pass by. Chances are, you'll be able to make the Loner feel more comfortable around you and others—and if so, he'll be grateful, and you will be able to exchange ideas more effectively.
- *Discover the Loner's special skills*. Is it his creativity? His agility with numbers? His writing? Taking the time to discover these skills can help you and your department produce better work, design better brochures, prepare more creative presentations. Quiet does not mean inept. Take the time to find out what the Loner can contribute.

Premium Blends

- *The Loner–Thespian*. This blend may sound like an oxymoron, but it isn't. How many times have you read the celebrity interview of the famous actor who confesses, "Deep down, I'm really shy"? We never believe the superstar who says this, but we should. Getting into character is a safe way for the Loner to come out of his shell. Likewise, in the workplace, low-key and reserved people often psych themselves up before the big meeting or presentation, with good results.

- *The Loner–A Student.* The fantasy: Imagine that everyone promises to leave you alone and you get to crawl into your cave and hide out and produce excellent work. And when you emerge, everyone fawns over your results, worships you, tells you you're a genius, and lets you get back to your work.

Poisonous Blend

- *The Loner–Player.* This type is quiet, isolated, and unassuming at work—and keeps very busy after hours. Good at keeping secrets (who would the Loner–Player tell?), this type, sadly, is attractive prey to the sexual predators in the office.

THE CHEERLEADER

A merry heart maketh a cheerful countenance.

—BIBLE, PROVERBS

Didn't you ever wonder where Cheerleaders stored such boundless energy? How they stayed so limber? And how they seemed to live for one purpose alone—to energize others and encourage them on to victory? While the majority of the student body considered organized cheering at football games to be a necessary evil, the cheerleading hopefuls took it seriously, starting with tryouts. Winning a spot on the squad would guarantee visibility and recognition right along with the team.

The workforce, like your high school football team, needs Cheerleaders, too: to rally a department or team when the competition is a few market share points ahead; to muster the strength to complete a project on time and within budget; and to harness the energy needed to raise morale when it has gone south. The Cheerleader in the workplace is the Energizer Bunny who keeps on moving and keeps others moving.

Today's workplace Cheerleaders aren't limited to business matters. They're busy gathering supporters and players for the company's softball league and can't fathom that you'd rather be somewhere else next Friday afternoon than at Goddard Park wearing the new departmental sweatshirt and a pair of old jeans. Their enthusiasm is unmistakable, if a bit insistent. As a result, sometimes their efforts and their optimism go underappreciated.

Workplace Cheerleaders are as enthusiastic on paper as they are in person. They pepper their memos with superlatives: "Thank you *so very* much for the time you spent clarifying the new project. I am *extremely excited* about the opportunity to work on it with the team and *very, very* eager to move forward. I know the results will be *fantastic.* . . ." This excessive zeal can detract from the impact of the message.

The same holds true for the Cheerleader's presentations, which tend also to be filled with extravagant words and claims. They often exaggerate the results of their recommendations with overly positive language. In short, their promises and optimism sometimes sound too good to be true.

Yet Cheerleaders *are* there for you when you need them. When you lose your backbone after a colleague dumps work on you or takes credit for work you did, it is the Cheerleader who can coach you to stand up for yourself and straighten out the situation. Yes, it is the Cheerleader who helps bolster your courage so you can get up the nerve to march right into the offending colleague's office and work things out. What's more, these hardy types help *themselves* out of jams like this, too.

Wouldn't it be nice if there were a bit of the Cheerleader in us all?

The Cheerleader's Communication Style

- The Cheerleader's primary power comes from an ever-present vocal and physical vitality. Such verbal and non-verbal animation adds up to unabashed enthusiasm. And while more quiet sorts may not always agree with such a show of spirit, they nonetheless stand back and admire the Cheerleader's eternal perkiness.

- Physical agility and attractiveness, so natural to the Cheerleader, contribute to the physical presence this type creates. The Cheerleader is not shy about getting everyone's attention.

- The Cheerleader also has a keen sense of timing, knowing when to encourage, when to celebrate, when to shout, and when to put the pom-poms down and be quiet and wait.

The Cheerleader's Strengths

- *Loyalty.* One of the Cheerleader's remarkable qualities is allegiance. Cheerleaders give their all when they "root, root, root for the home team." Loyalty and spirit are qualities less frequently seen these days in the workplace. Such loyalty is a refreshing contrast and doesn't go unnoticed.

- *Energy and enthusiasm.* Especially if focused on important projects. The adept Cheerleader can discern what projects require a boost in spirit, and then give it. Departments and teammates are obliged to the ever pumped-up

Cheerleader who picks up flagging morale—and the Cheerleader's timely efforts may just help the company's bottom line.

- *Motivational skill.* Already a spirited believer, the Cheerleader can keep productivity up and help spread the good word and deeds of the company within and without. The Cheerleader's passion and enthusiasm makes him a popular figure and admired coach.

What Undermines the Cheerleader's Success?

- *Overstating a situation.* Cheerleaders, with their inherent zest, tend to exaggerate. The result can be overly dramatic reporting of a situation. Or being viewed as obnoxious rather than enthusiastic. Their credibility can suffer.
- *Overreacting.* Because Cheerleaders tend to be in a constantly revved-up state, they have difficulty toning down reactions to a situation so that their reason will be more plausible to the boss than their ranting. Cheerleaders tend to overtly reveal their emotional extremes—wild happiness when all's well and jitters when all's not.
- *Overreliance on superlatives.* Cheerleaders need to choose their words with care. In their enthusiasm, they may sprinkle superlatives too freely in their memos, meetings, and presentations. Superlatives and qualifiers, while intended to intensify a point, end up diluting its genuineness. It's less powerful to say "that most incredible campaign really, really surprised the competition" than "our campaign astounded the competition."

If Your Boss or Colleague Is a Cheerleader

- *Get on board.* A positive attitude can only do you good, as long as you don't go overboard. Remember that enthusiasm can be contagious and helpful in the workplace.
- *When you're down, turn to the Cheerleader for support.* When you are worried or concerned about work, let the Cheerleader mentor and motivate you. That's what Cheerleaders like to do, and what they do so naturally.
- *Feel grateful that you don't work for/with a cynical curmudgeon.* Cheerleaders are naturally effusive. Enjoy their enthusiasm and praise—then strive to live up to and even exceed it with results.

Premium Blends

- *The Cheerleader–Jock.* There's a reason they worked so well together in high school. The Cheerleader's enthusiasm combined with the Jock's stamina, patience, and persistence can pay big dividends over the long term.
- *The Cheerleader–Geek.* Big enthusiasm fused with big ideas. Okay, we admit that this combination produced Doctors Jekyll and Frankenstein, but they were the exceptions. Many of the pioneers of the Internet revolution were incredibly excitable, energetic people with wild ideas, tireless focus, and the ability to sell those ideas to others (particularly investors!).
- *The Cheerleader–Class President.* Since the Cheerleader is often supporting the company's agenda and not necessarily driving it, combining forces with the Class Presi-

dent's leadership skills makes for an influential player in the workplace.

Poisonous Blend

- *The Cheerleader–Gossip.* This type is the classic two-face, supporting the boss and colleagues . . . and then saying malicious things about them behind their backs.

THE STRAIGHT ARROW

Character is higher than intellect.

—RALPH WALDO EMERSON

In the movies and on TV, the swaggering Rebels got all the attention. But in real life, high school was made up mostly of Straight Arrow students: good kids who played by the rules, got decent grades, were liked by both peers and faculty, looked good, and maybe even played a good game of tennis or sang in the choir. Hollywood may have taught us to worship the Rebels but when there was trouble at home or in school we relied on the Straight Arrows for friendship and support. When Straight Arrows were asked about future plans they always gave a straight answer. "I'm going into the navy and then on to nursing school" or "I'm going to law school and then I hope to join my dad's firm."

As adults, Straight Arrows are good colleagues in the workplace. They are trustworthy, loyal, likable, and reliable. They are professional and competitive but never ruthless. These are not the folks who get caught up in politics and intrigues; they don't have to. They do as much good as they can, and as little harm as they must. In short, they make the world go round.

Look at the Straight Arrow, an assistant manager at a luxury hotel. Days, nights, and weekends are spent fixing problems. When a guest is unhappy, it's the hotel's fault—even if it is not the hotel's fault. The Straight Arrow stays steady, focused, and calm when dealing with guests, underlings, and the hotel's general manager. The Straight Arrow doesn't care whose fault it is and isn't interested in assigning blame: The objective is to fix the problem and make the guest happy.

Straight Arrows assume 100 percent responsibility, get results, don't chew anybody out or pass the buck, and turn negatives into positives. With a Straight Arrow, what you see is what you get.

The Straight Arrow's Communication Style

- The Straight Arrow's primary power comes from being real, genuine, authentic.
- The Straight Arrow doesn't strut around like a peacock. Years of getting things right and being rewarded for it have made them comfortable in their own skin. They communicate plainly, gracefully, and confidently.
- The Straight Arrow speaks and writes in a manner that is not too loud, not too timid.
- The Straight Arrow follows the rules. But this doesn't mean she isn't fun. Straight Arrows can appreciate a good joke and incorporate appropriate humor into their transactions with others.

The Straight Arrow's Strengths

- *Reliability.* The Straight Arrow always gets the job done. Bosses know that when they hire a Straight Arrow, they won't have to worry about hovering over shoulders and cracking the whip.
- *Fit.* There are few environments where a Straight Arrow won't thrive. They are smart, easy to get along with, and eager to do a good job. Straight Arrows are amazingly adaptable. They pay close attention to the prevailing culture and learn quickly how to blend in. They neither stand out too much nor blend in to the point of invisibility; they get it just right.
- *Endurance.* Straight Arrows are more likely to try to work things out than stomp their feet in protest or quit. If summer school is what it takes to get into the good college, then that's what is done. That canoeing trip will just have to wait. Likewise, if getting promoted to the next level means reporting to the less-than-beloved regional manager or moving the family to Houston, then that's what is done.

What Undermines the Straight Arrow's Success

- *Risk aversion.* The Straight Arrow has done pretty darn well without having to stick her neck out. Still, risk aversion can be the Straight Arrow's Achilles' heel. It can keep this competent achiever from reaching for the stars and fulfilling her true potential. It can also keep her from getting the recognition and rewards she has already earned through hard work.

- *Excessive accommodation.* The Straight Arrow's reliability and integrity are assets to any organization, but these qualities can be irresistible to opportunists at the bottom of the class. The Straight Arrow is an attractive target for manipulation precisely because she doesn't like to fight or make waves. Straight Arrows must stand up for themselves.

- *Conventional thinking.* Straight Arrows need to be careful that they don't spend all of their time thinking inside the box, or they may find themselves hitting a ceiling in their careers. Ambitious Straight Arrows sometimes have to unlearn the skills that brought them success. They may have made following instructions an art form, but need to evolve from order taker to idea maker.

If Your Boss or Colleague Is a Straight Arrow

- *Count your blessings.* If your boss or colleague is a Straight Arrow, you have the privilege to work alongside or for a person with integrity and strong, homegrown values. You'll find it comfortable to be around this type. No game playing. No politics. No backstabbing.

- *Join their team.* Because Straight Arrows do their job responsibly, working with them is usually rewarding. They'll do their share, making it easy for you to contribute yours.

- *Encourage and support initiative and risk taking.* If your boss is a Straight Arrow, your department or business unit will probably work up to its potential but not exceed it. That's because Straight Arrows are risk averse. If you provide support and detailed follow-through, you can encourage the Straight Arrow to stretch, and possibly grab the gold ring.

Premium Blends

- *The Straight Arrow–Go-getter.* In this case, the sum is even greater than the parts (and both parts are quite good). When a trustworthy, loyal, likable Straight Arrow gets a dose of the Go-getter's courage and umph, greatness is within reach.
- *The Straight Arrow–Activist.* This type is slow to anger, but unafraid to fight for what she considers fair and decent and right. Think Eleanor Roosevelt.

Poisonous Blend

- *The Straight Arrow–Know-it-all.* This type is sanctimonious, smug, and puritanical. A didactic, *Roberts Rules of Order*–quoting, corporate handbook aficionado. And did we mention she's no fun, either?

THE GO-GETTER

I am looking for a dare-to-be-great situation.
—JOHN CUSAK AS LLOYD DOBBLER IN *SAY ANYTHING*

You remember the Go-getter from high school. Not necessarily smarter, better looking, or more likable than the others. But the Go-getter had nerve. Make that king-sized nerve. The Go-getter girl had her eye on the captain of the football team, went right up to him at the pep rally, and told him so. And the Go-getter boy decided he was taking the prettiest girl to the prom, marched right up to her after school while she and her friends were waiting for the bus, looked her square in the eyes, and asked for a date.

Of course you resented them. What made *her* think she could win the team captain's affection by simply walking up to him and telling him she admired him? And what made *him* think he was qualified to take the goddess to the prom? But you secretly envied them, too. How on earth did they pull it off?

At work, most employees operate within the boundaries of their job descriptions. Not the Go-getter. For example, Go-getter

Julie is the bar manager for a steakhouse that's part of a big chain. The general manager at the restaurant—Julie's boss—is in a panic: The chain's regional vice president is paying a visit today. While touring the restaurant, the VP and GM stop at the bar area. "How's business?" asks the VP. "It's good," says Julie, "but it could be great." She then offers several ideas for overhauling the bar appetizer menu and adding some trendy new cocktails. The VP is impressed with the Go-getter's moxie. Behind the fake smile plastered across the face of the general manager, the blood is draining. Six months from now Julie will be working at corporate headquarters in Boston. The GM will keep doing things by the numbers.

The Go-getter is full of sass and spunk. Call it chutzpah. In the business world as in school, the bold, the daring, and the fearless get to the top the fastest. They are not nine-to-five types or quitters.

The Go-getter's Communication Style

- What Go-getters may lack in physical stature they make up for in sheer nerve. Their fearlessness and forthrightness create enormous height and might. They are not afraid to look you in the eye. Or get in your face.
- Like the Jocks, Go-getters walk tall, as if to say, "I'm someone you want to know."
- Go-getters romance audiences with bold talk and bolder promises. They may even dare to swear—often. Their voices are loud and confident.
- Clothes tend to play up how positively Go-getters think of themselves, how confident they are about their ability to meet and match any situation.

The Go-getter's Strengths

- *Sounding like an expert.* For the Go-getter, this behavior is not only common sense but also common practice. While a lot of people behave like order takers, reporting to work and doing what they're told, Go-getters behave like idea makers. Their boldness and confidence help them sell their ideas and inspire others to do more.

- *Displaying a confident point of view.* The object of the Go-getter's attention would never tolerate a stammering I'm-not-sure-if-you're-free-this-Saturday-but I-was-wondering . . . appeal. Same at work. It doesn't matter if the Go-getter's opinions on a subject are a mirror reflection of the boss's or if she has a different take altogether. Either way, the Go-getter is never wishy-washy.

- *Staying the course.* Go-getters rarely back down or reverse their position. Nine times out of ten the boss will accept her recommendation if she has a proven track record. On those occasions when the boss disagrees, the smart Go-getter knows how to respectfully and graciously disagree with a superior, and pledge to complete the assignment the way the boss wants it done.

What Undermines the Go-getter's Success

- *Overshooting.* Once Go-getters discover that people will listen to them because they come across as experts, it's tempting to claim expertise in all areas. For the ex-

tremely clever Go-getter—and the extremely brave—
this strategy will pay high dividends. But it will also
make him a lot of enemies. When the Go-getter becomes an "expert" in Bob's area, and Susan's, and
Mikal's—and gets himself a promotion—Bob, Susan,
and Mikal will be lining up to bring him down.

- *Forgetting who is boss.* There's a fine line between giving
  the boss your opinion and giving him orders. The Go-
  getter needs to be careful not to talk to a superior as
  though she is the college professor and the boss an in-
  coming first-year student.

- *Misreading the audience.* Go-getters are sometimes slow to
  realize that some people prefer a less assertive, less flam-
  boyant approach. Go-getters can be inflexible about al-
  tering their own style for the situation or the sale.

If Your Boss or Colleague Is a Go-getter

- *Understand that you are on your own.* Go-getters usually
  do not intend to help or harm you; normally, they don't
  even *see* you. It's not personal, it's just that the Go-getter
  looks in only one direction: up. And not just one rung
  higher up the ladder but several. If the Go-getter is your
  boss, you will probably be treated respectfully, but it is
  unlikely that you will be mentored or groomed. Go-
  getters are not interested in subordinates. Consequently,
  you'll need to take responsibility for crafting your image
  and getting recognition for your work. You'll have to
  "get caught doing something good," because the Go-
  getter will not be championing your cause. If the Go-

getter is your peer, you will probably be jealous. Get over it. You can resent the Go-getter and get left in the dust, or make a friend who is going places.

- *Ride his coattails.* If you can make yourself useful, and visible, to the Go-getter, he may take you along for the ride. But be forewarned: You've got your work cut out for you. The Go-getter is a lone wolf who does not necessarily value or reward loyalty. A year from now it's just as likely the Go-getter in your department will be working for a new company. Don't take it personally; loyalty just isn't his strong suit.

Premium Blends

- *The Go-getter–Class President.* Mix the boldness, bravery, and charm of the Go-getter with the political acumen and leadership skills of the Class President and you're on the CEO track.
- *The Go-getter–Straight Arrow.* With this type you have a blend of courage and consistency. This combination has the rare ability to make friends on the way to the top— and to get results.

Poisonous Blend

- *The Go-getter–Prima Donna.* These are people with really, really big ideas who insist on having their way: a total-itarian dictator in the making. Just rent *Working Girl* some weekend and see how Sigourney Weaver plays out this role to her character's demise.

THE CLASS PRESIDENT

Ask not what your country can do for you.
Ask what you can do for your country.

—JOHN F. KENNEDY

Let's start with a test question: Choose the pair of words that is related in the same way as the pair in capital letters.

LUNCH TABLE was to **HIGH SCHOOL STUDENT** as

A. uniform is to athlete
B. flag is to country
C. colors are to gang
D. military branch is to soldier
E. all of the above

The correct answer is E. At most high schools, the lunch table represented the ultimate pledge of allegiance. Where and with whom you sat broadcast everything about you—your grades, your interests, your popularity, and your potential. Most students picked a table (or were granted admission to one) their first year and stayed for four. Except the Class President. A born leader and natural politician, the Class President moved effortlessly from table to table, from one group to another, year after year. On Monday the Jocks made room at their table. On Tuesday the Geeks pulled up an extra chair. On Wednesday the Rebels shrugged, and said, "Sure, you can join us." The Class President wasn't always the most dynamic or charismatic person at school, but he had what really mattered— an easy likability and the ability to motivate others.

When the school principal announced that the Math department was going to be shrunk by several teachers and courses, it was the Class President who appeared before the Board of Education with statistics on how standardized math test scores in their district had risen over the past five years. "Why would any school want to take a step backward?" he pleaded. They worked out a compromise.

At work, Class Presidents are up to the same sort of productive problem solving. The Class President who has risen to become the national sales director still stays close to what is happening in the field with forty district managers: providing weekly motivational tips on how to handle resistant or rude customers; writing personal thank-yous to the top monthly performers; coaching those performing less well; and working on plans at headquarters that will more efficiently provide the field with information needed to sell more.

Class Presidents are energy personified. They are usually "up," brimming with optimism and full of plans. They not only believe in the possibilities, they create them.

It's no wonder that in the workplace the Class President rises quickly. Class Presidents are great at organizing assignments and people, inspiring confidence, and delivering results. A lot of people say they like working in teams when deep down they detest it. The Class President likes to work in teams and means it.

Class Presidents are real leaders. They rarely have to seize power. Because they are smart, do a good job, and treat people with respect, power comes to *them*.

The Class President's Communication Style

- Class Presidents communicate in a style that is open, sincere, and generous, making them eminently likable.
- Class Presidents talk *to* you, not *at* you. They don't scream, because they don't have to.
- The Class President does not talk just to be heard but speaks when he has something to say.
- This type often listens well, which is why people relate and are willing to follow.
- Their primary communications power comes from personal credibility and conviction. For example, when Ronald Reagan was president, critics who disagreed with his policies often said they respected and admired the man.

The Class President's Strengths

- *Egalitarianism.* Class Presidents can communicate and get along with anyone—a gift at any age.
- *Competence.* They get the job done. They know they can do it. This is why top management keeps giving them more responsibility and more promotions.

- *Confidence.* Competence builds confidence, which makes a Class President completely at ease when asking to sit down at a lunch table inhabited by weight lifters or people with pierced eyebrows and purple hair. Or the corporate CEO.
- *Multitasking.* Class Presidents can handle long to-do lists. With their ability to focus, they can execute on several fronts at once, and are good at mobilizing others to pitch in, too.

What Undermines the Class President's Success

- *Power hunger.* Some leaders overreach and try to take on more and more and more. Enemies will be made. This may not matter to the leader who soars all the way to the top. But when you are in the middle and making enemies, the folks above you will probably hear about it.
- *Arrogance.* When people look up to you and sing your praises, it's easy to get a swollen head. Be careful. Leadership is about responsibility and restraint. Exercise both.
- *Waffling.* Some leaders try to please everyone and end up pleasing no one. This happens to Class Presidents, corporate leaders, and even heads of state. Don't be seduced by the need to please. Stand for something and stand your ground.

If Your Boss or Colleague Is a Class President

- *Volunteer to lead a team.* Especially if your boss is the Class President. By doing so, you'll show you're a team player. And maybe you'll end up winning the MVP.
- *Consider yourself fortunate.* Class Presidents are rarely wishy-washy. They won't let the department flounder long before coming up with a plan. It's better to be in a lifeboat that has life vests. Class Presidents never desert the ship.
- *Make your skills visible.* Class Presidents have a full agenda and they can't accomplish everything all alone. They need to delegate—so show them what you can offer.

Premium Blends

- *Class President–A Student.* Likability and logic combine in this type. Aristotle claimed that to be truly persuasive, a person had to show intellect, character, and goodwill. Bingo!
- *Class President–Activist.* This type can be a force to be contended with. The power to lead. The power to empathize. The power to execute and get things done.

Poisonous Blend

- *Class President–Prima Donna.* This type seduces and betrays. The charisma reels us in, but in the end the Prima Donna's narcissism says it's all about me, not you.

THE THESPIAN

It takes me more than three weeks to prepare an impromptu speech.

—MARK TWAIN

The curtain came down on the school's production of *Guys and Dolls* at the end of junior year, but the Thespian was still in character a year later, affecting the accent of the 1930s New York gangster who is trying to sound smart: "It is twelve-oh-seven in the afternoon and I am standing in the lunch line. I am much surprised to see the same old grilled cheese sandwich on the menu. I often hear rumors that the grilled cheese sandwich is a healthful and delicious sandwich, but the rumors are untrue. For as I look at this sandwich wrapped in tinfoil under the heat lamp, the way it looks back at me makes me very nervous indeed."

Behind the glitter, lights, and flashy costumes was a lot of hard work. It took three months of rehearsals to master the dialect. (No wonder the Thespian refused to retire the character.) It took courage to stand up in front of a packed auditorium and deliver a monologue or sing a solo. In fact, it took courage to try out for a part at all, given the possibility of being rejected.

At work, the Thespian may be slightly less dramatic, but very much in character. Some Thespians actually invent a work character for themselves. They decide they want their co-workers to think of them as the Executive, or the Eccentric, or the Intellectual. They rehearse and prepare exhaustively for the role, asking themselves, *How does an Intellectual dress, talk, write? What's the voice? How's the posture? Who played the Intellectual in the movies?* They work to get every character trait *nailed*. The really good actors come across as believable, making it difficult to tell who the real person is behind the mask they've donned. But the bad ones come off as melodramatic—their "performances" sappy and canned. Just like some of the amateur productions you sat through in school.

The Thespian's Communication Style

- Thespians get their power from their ability to perform—to become something or someone other than who they are, in voice, body, and attitude.
- The Thespian communicates with flair. Her writing, presentation, and speaking is colorful, animated, energetic, and dramatic.
- The Thespian pays attention to his voice. This is not to say that all Thespians try to talk like Shakespearean actors, but they pay attention to how they sound, and they work hard to get their voice right.
- Thespians love attention. Their clothing, their words, their memos, and their presentations are designed to attract it.

The Thespian's Strengths

- *Bravery.* It takes a lot of courage to stand up on a stage at seventeen . . . or forty-five. Many speakers are terrified of the audience; the Thespian actually draws energy from the audience and converts that energy into power—*personal* power.
- *Improvisation.* The best Thespians can go in and out of character, and invent new ones, on the spot. Whatever the situation calls for, talented Thespians adapt.
- *Presentation skills.* Thespians take their presentations very seriously. They accurately view presenting as the craft it is. They train: they are happy to take public-speaking classes, they rehearse exhaustively, they memorize their "lines," they incorporate theatrical tricks (like well-timed silence) into their presentations.

What Undermines the Thespian's Success

- *Spotlight grabbing.* The Thespian's evil twin is the Prima Donna, who steals the scene from everyone else in the room. Co-workers and bosses—*especially* bosses!—don't appreciate being upstaged.
- *Exhausting the audience.* Thespians have tremendous energy and enthusiasm, and may come on too strong. They need to remember that every play has an intermission and every sitcom has a commercial. The audience enjoys a break.
- *Stage panic.* Some Thespians panic or melt down when they are not given sufficient rehearsal time, or they for-

get their lines "onstage," or they are asked to talk without first being handed a script. The Thespian must learn
to stay lucid, loose, and spontaneous, because not every
moment in life can be rehearsed for or stage-managed.

- *Artistic Temperament.* In the workplace, people who fancy
  themselves Artistes, may be moody and difficult. Thespians need to take care of their own needs while not
  abusing or ignoring others in the process.

If Your Boss or Colleague Is a Thespian

- *Appreciate his performance.* Approval is as vital as is
  breathing to the Thespian. Nod in acknowledgment.
  Smile in return. Listen. And, if your boss is a Thespian,
  be certain to never, ever upstage him.
- *Study their presentation skills.* Thespians can be powerful
  presenters. They know how to sound, how to inflect,
  how to walk, when to pause.
- *Coach them through their stage fright.* Before a major meeting or in front of senior management, it's likely they'll
  have stage jitters. They'll be grateful for your calming
  influence.

Premium Blends

- *Thespian–Activist.* This type puts it all together: passion
  for a cause, and the stage delivery to make it compelling
  to others. An environmental activist in Northern California advocates for protection of ancient redwoods by
  walking directly into logging sites, stripping, and reading

poetry to the stunned loggers. She calls her approach "goddess-based, nude Buddhist guerilla poetry." (We're not making this up.) The Thespian–Activist attracts attention to herself, of course, but also to her important cause.

- *Thespian–A Student.* This type combines the desire to be the best with the willingness to put in the hours and hard work to pull it off. How do you get to Carnegie Hall? This blend knows: Practice, practice, practice.

Poisonous Blends

- *Thespian–Prima Donna.* Give us a break! Each of these types by itself is an attention seeker. Both adore entrances and center stage. It would be hard to find a corporate stage large enough for this blend to perform well on.

THE ACTIVIST

If you're outraged at conditions, then you can't possibly be free or happy until you devote all your time to changing them and do nothing but that.

—CÉSAR CHÁVEZ

They set up tables outside the cafeteria. "Right-wing military thugs in Chile are unjustly imprisoning Juan Gomez! Our goal is to send one thousand postcards to his prison. Please, take one of these postcards. All you have to do is sign it and mail it. We want the thugs to know that the world is watching! Please, won't you help?"

They volunteered at the hospital, picked up stray animals, fed the homeless, passed out leaflets on curbing environmental waste; searched for holiness in the unholy. In the 1960s, they marched for civil rights or became Peace Corps volunteers; in the '70s, they protested the war in Vietnam; in the '80s, they fought Apartheid; in the '90s, they protested against globalization; and in the twenty-first century, they continue to fight for justice.

While everyone else was fretting over prom dates and pimples, the Activist was out to change the world for the better. The Activist's passion, conviction, and concern never wavered.

All grown up, workplace Activists still champion causes, fighting for the little guy, just as they did for the endangered or the embattled. "Can someone help me understand why the top executives at this company make 160 times what the lowest-paid employee does?" the Activist asks. The best ones do more than simply point out injustice; they do something about it. The boss who goes to bat for the assistant who isn't being paid fairly. Or the executive who has the courage to stand up to the policy council by stating that it's unfair to change everyone's status to part-time so the company no longer has to provide insurance benefits. Or the administrative assistant who marches into the president's office with a petition signed by 432 employees against the company's building the addition right next to the pond that is home to a flock of mallard ducks.

Activists operate in a variety of styles. One is an aggressive style, not hesitating to take up a sign and loudly march in the company's parking lot. Another is a more docile manner, working behind the scenes, writing letters and circulating a petition to achieve the same results. Both are passionate and focused.

The Activist's Communication Style

- The Activist's source of power is his moral authority. Activists are unfazed and unimpressed by title, power, seniority, or other credentials. A mail clerk with conviction and character will get the Activist's respect more readily than a slippery CEO.
- The Activist's fire fuels an assertive communication style. Activists usually speak, write, and present themselves with energy, enthusiasm, and feistiness.

- The Activist is about one thing: justice. The communications tactic employed to achieve justice: persuasion. The Activist verbally grabs others by their hearts, minds, or elsewhere.
- The Activist communicates confidence. He is emboldened and empowered by the courage of his convictions, and isn't ashamed to show it.
- The best Activists communicate dignity. Moral certainty and purpose can be seen on their faces, in their posture. Take a good look at the actor Sidney Poitier, who has fought his whole life for the things he believes in.

The Activist's Strengths

- *Sales expertise.* The Activist sells ideas the way a traditional salesperson sells copiers or cars. He is all about persuasion. The Activist has a strong point of view and wants others to embrace it. Robert F. Kennedy employed his amazing writing, speaking, and personal presentation skills to "sell" justice to the American people. It worked.
- *Conviction.* The turtle makes progress only by sticking its neck out. Likewise, the Activist makes progress—and inspires others—by taking a stand. Whether it's to create a stronger diversity council at work or to find homes for a litter of pups, Activists don't rest until the job is done. They believe one person *can* make a difference.
- *Leadership potential.* Activists engender loyalty and trust from those around them. It takes guts to organize every-

one at the garment factory and start a union; no wonder the Activist becomes its first president.

- *Intelligence.* The Activist's intelligence informs her speaking, writing, and personal presentation style. Because Activists care so deeply about their issues, they usually do their homework, and can speak logically and even eloquently about the issues.
- *Empathy.* When they don't overdo it, Activists are a refreshing antidote to a sometimes callous workplace.
- *Example.* The most inspiring Activists practice what they preach.

What Undermines the Activist's Success

- *Fighting the wrong battles.* When the Activist, the issue, and the moment collide, as it did when Lenin came to power after the Russian Revolution, history is made. But Activists have to be smart about when and how they strike. After a round of layoffs, the Activist who still has a job is ill advised to march into the boss's office and demand raises for everyone who made the cut.
- *Fighting too many battles at once.* César Chávez founded and led the first successful farm workers' union in U.S. history. He forged a national support coalition of unions, church groups, students, minorities, and consumers. He led a successful five-year strike and boycott against California grape growers. This takes tremendous skill and determination. But it also takes focus. Chávez may very well have believed people should also drive

electric cars, recycle, and stop eating red meat. But he was smart enough not to dilute his message by championing too many causes at once.

- *Self-righteousness.* The Activist is sometimes tempted to cast those with differing views as morally inferior. Lynn from Operations is a vegan who does not eat meat, chicken, eggs, or cheese. Lynn's colleague Jeri from Accounting still eats meat, chicken, eggs, and cheese. Jeri does not deserve to be scolded or shamed during lunch. She just wants to eat her bologna sandwich in peace. The company cafeteria is big enough for both of them.
- *Discomfort with Dissension.* Differences of opinion help businesses ultimately make the right decisions, manufacture the best products, and offer employees the best benefits packages. The Activist needs to realize that differing points of view, dialogue, and compromise are critical for reaching the best solutions.
- *Intolerance.* Some Activists are so certain they're right that they lose their ability to entertain the possibility they might be wrong—and show no interest in checking.

If Your Boss or Colleague Is an Activist

- *Fasten your seat belt.* You'll probably need to go along for the ride, at least to hear them out.
- *Avoid land mines.* While there's little upside to debating politics with people at work, and the subject is best avoided, you have a right not to be bullied or bowled over by a co-worker's views. Being around Activists in

the workplace can be both a blessing and a curse. A blessing if their cause is just (and you agree with it), and a curse if you don't.

- *Advise them not to break the law.* Henry David Thoreau refused to pay his taxes, and his civil disobedience resulted in jail time. Try to find an intervention inside the law to help the Activist make his point.

Premium Blends

- *Activist–A Student.* This type gets taken seriously. It combines the intellect to thoroughly understand an issue and the passion to do something about it.
- *Activist–Jock.* Moral muscle is on display with this type, who pulls together the ingredients necessary to accomplish change: conscience, compassion, and the connections to get results.

Poisonous Blend

- *Activist–Complainer.* This type is hard to be around. His whining and nagging grate on everyone's nerves. Though the cause might be just and the need for change real, the style of the Activist–Complainer works against his cause. Ultimately this combination can do more harm than good.

THE UNDERACHIEVER

If you're coasting, you're going downhill.

—L. W. PIERSON

The senior-year term paper on *War and Peace* was torture for everyone in Mr. Cekota's English class . . . except for the Underachiever, who read only the first and last chapters of the book, wrote the paper before school on the morning it was due, and was awarded a B.

The Underachiever was competent at everything and seemingly excellent at nothing—and a master at winging it. He could study algebra for twenty hours and get an A+; or study for two hours, watch TV for eighteen, and get a B. The teachers' comments on his report cards were always the same: "Works below potential."

The Underachiever: a Porsche stuck in neutral.

Two decades later, the Underachiever is still coasting along. It's June 1—the day of dread at Gargantua, Inc., the world's largest corporate conglomerate. Every year promotions are announced on this day. The Underachiever, an office manager in the field sales division, has been checking hourly for the e-mail announcement from the CEO. At 3:30 P.M., it arrives. Frenzied clicking of the mouse. The hunt is under way. Scroll up. Scroll down. Eyes darting. "Where the hell am I?" asks the Underachiever. The list is double-checked, then triple-checked. The blood starts to boil. The pity party begins.

"Why do I keep getting passed over!" fumes the Underachiever . . . who has a point. Neophyte office managers from around the company are sent to Field Sales to learn the tricks of the trade from the master. "You're as smart as people two or even three grades higher in this division," said the VP at the holiday party. "You could do anything you wanted if you set your mind to it." The Underachiever deletes the long-awaited promotions announcement memo from the in box, huffs, and storms out, moaning, "What do I have to do to get promoted around here?"

The answer: finish school.

The Underachiever is six credits shy of a bachelor's degree. The VP has been saying for seven years that promotion to the next level requires a degree. The VP has also reminded him that Gargantua, Inc. offers 100 percent tuition reimbursement. The VP has been rooting for the Underachiever all along. But at a certain point, she refuses to take responsibility for the Underachiever's happiness or success—the Underachiever must do that himself.

Raw ingredients and potential, no matter how fabulous, will not pay the rent. Nor will they, alone, bring professional satisfaction. In the workplace, Underachievers who keep waiting for their potential to happen *to* them (instead of making it happen *for* themselves) are in big trouble. In short, the Underachiever may have amazing potential, but this type is in a serious race against the clock:

those who never quite manage to get their act together eventually collapse, like a soufflé left to stand too long.

There's only one real distinction between the Overachiever and the Underachiever: discipline. The Underachiever is all about being clever, getting by. The Overachiever is all about being talented and getting results. The difference between the Overachiever and the Underachiever is the difference between lightning and the lightning bug, to paraphrase Mark Twain. It's the difference between picking up the guitar and strumming a pop tune by ear versus taking classical guitar lessons and practicing every day for ninety minutes.

The Underachiever's Communication Style

- Underachievers draw on their natural expertise and personality—their charisma—as a source of power.
- Underachievers are famously good talkers, writers, and presenters.
- They are natural conversationalists. (They've got to be talented talkers since they didn't spend hours preparing.)
- When bored, which is often, Underachievers move about lethargically; their body language says to others that they are uninspired, that they are bored, that their batteries are running low.

What Are the Underachiever's Strengths?

- *Quick-wittedness.* Underachievers are naturally bright. After decades of not doing the homework assignment, they've had to learn to think quickly on their feet.

- *Charm.* They get away with their unpreparedness because teachers and bosses are seduced by the Underachiever's innate intelligence, wit, and charm. The boss is often secretly rooting for the Underachiever to work up to his potential.
- *Self-deprecation.* Underachievers manage other people's expectations of themselves downward. This increases their likability and is a refreshing antidote to the self-promoting atmosphere of many workplaces. In addition, competitors and critics often underestimate the Underachiever . . . but they do so at their own risk.
- *Limitless potential.* In the right environment, Underachievers blossom. There was always one teacher who saw the Underachiever's potential and cajoled excellence out of this student. Likewise, the boss who creates the right work environment will be awestruck (and delighted) when the chrysalis Underachiever metamorphoses into the A Student butterfly.

What Undermines the Underachiever's Success?

- *Lack of discipline.* Or, to be less charitable, good old-fashioned *laziness.* Underachievers are always clever enough to get by. But as they age, they find it's easier to actually do the work rather than bluff their way through one situation after another.
- *Ducking responsibility.* Underachievers condition people not to expect excellence from them, yet are disappointed when colleagues no longer demand it. They must take responsibility for their own happiness, and for the real-

ization of their own potential. Underachievers often wait for opportunities to shine when they have the skills to *create* such opportunities for themselves.

- *Mischief-making.* Underachievers sometimes become angry and frustrated because their songs get trapped in their throat. When bright people are bored, or underutilized, they can grow bitter. They often get cynical. Then they get into mischief.

Premium Blends

- *The Underachiever–Activist.* When this blend is thrust into an extraordinary situation the Underachiever–Activist rises to the occasion. Vocational-school graduate Lech Walesa was an ordinary guy holding an ordinary job in the Gdansk shipyards until a clash between workers and the government became the spark that ignited his potential, compelling him to organize the Solidarity trade-union movement in Poland.
- *The Underachiever–Party Animal.* This type has been in a constant state of networking—and doesn't even realize it. Eminently likable, utterly nonthreatening, and supremely well connected, this type has scores of friends. When the Underachiever–Party Animal wants to change jobs, or pitch new business, or show up at the grand opening, these valuable relationships can be leveraged for success.

Poisonous Blend

- *The Underachiever–Cheater.* The Underachiever has a decision to make: He has an angel on one shoulder who dares him to be great. But on the other shoulder stands the Cheater, who dares him to take the easy way out. May he choose wisely. The Underachiever–Cheater is the ultimate tragedy: a shameful waste of talent.

THE BOTTOM OF THE CLASS

As iron is corroded by rust, your own mischief will consume you.

—DHAMMAPADA, THE SAYINGS OF THE BUDDHA

THE SNOB

Her voice is full of money.
—F. SCOTT FITZGERALD, *THE GREAT GATSBY*

Snobs *always* spent part of the summer somewhere else: at a beach house or their parents' place in the country. (The less wealthy but no less determined Snobs spread a beach towel out in the backyard and *pretended* to be in the Hamptons, on Martha's Vineyard, or at a country cottage.) Tales of their summer adventures intimated worldliness, a certain *savoir-faire*[1] that accompanied them everywhere they went, whether it was to French class or to Gym.

They had it all (or at least *acted* as if they did): breeding, wealth, privilege. And attitude. They did more, had more, traveled more, conversed about more, name-dropped more, and got on our nerves more.

Snobs don't actually talk *to* us as much as they talk *around* us.

---

[1] Snobs use this word a lot and know how to pronounce it.

And all conversational roads lead back to them. That first week back at school in September, the Snob, outfitted in crisp khaki, helpfully explained to classmates that Labor Day had passed and it was time to put the linen pants and white shoes away until next summer. The Snob delighted in knowing rules no one else knew— or cared to know.

In the modern workplace, the Snob has to be careful. Flaunting personal wealth or pointing out someone else's lack of it are just not acceptable. Being labeled elitist can be a professional death sentence. Instead of criticizing a colleague's poor fashion sense, shrewd Snobs advertise superiority in subtler ways. They often discuss their own excellent taste in cars, vacations, restaurants, clothes, books, TV shows, friends, etc. The comparison is implied, not stated.

The Snob breezes in to work on Tuesday morning, after the long President's Day weekend, sporting a golden tan. He walks into the conference room. Snobs enter rooms quietly but are anything but invisible. In fact, that tan is impossible *not* to notice. After all, he's wearing a crisp white shirt under the Armani suit. He looks around, and with a slight nod almost signals that the question be asked. "Where did you get such a great tan in the middle of February?"

"Oh," readily offers the Snob, in a slow, soft, yet calibrated and controlled tone. "My brother-in-law and sister flew to the Bahamas for the weekend—they have a friend who is a pilot—and so I tagged along." Stop. Silence. Let it sink in. The Snob knows you'll be back for more.

"Did you say you flew in a private plane?"

The Snob gladly elaborates.

You get the picture: the Snob's job is to remind others that they are *déclassé²*, er, ordinary. Snobs feel superior only when others feel inferior.

The Snob's Communication Style

- The Snob's power is drawn from title, expertise, physical presence, and personality.
- The Snob ruthlessly manages personal image and reputation. His appearance communicates cultivated taste, exclusivity, and status. He displays a strong stage presence.
- Snobs are often elegant writers and speakers. Their manners and mannerisms, in both speech and writing, are more formal than casual. The Snob's fussiness with language is an immediate giveaway. The Snob is determined to say it and write it exactly right. This *should* be a good thing. Most of us are less precise. Further, when someone speaks or writes well, it is usually a pleasure to hear what they have to say. But with the Snob, we experience the opposite reaction. Everything the Snob says is so . . . *affected*. If you've ever seen an etiquette expert on television or listened to one on the radio you'll know what we're talking about. The Snob grates because every pronouncement bears traces of judgment and condescension.
- The Snob is a master of understatement. In words, clothes, and physical comportment, he is measured. The

---

² Snobs use this word a lot, too, and know how to pronounce it.

Snob talks and speaks slowly. The Snob is *always* in control.

- Snobs project confidence. Whether the Snob went to an accredited finishing school or simply paid close attention, the effect is the same: The Snob is polished and secure.
- Snobs are often in the forefront of style. Though Snobs come in all sizes and shapes, the quality of their clothing (as well as the quantity) makes them look attractive and fashionable.

If Your Boss or Colleague Is A Snob

- *Refuse to be impressed.* The Snob gets the upper hand when you allow yourself to feel inferior. But what happens to the Snob's power if you refuse to follow the rules? If the Snob boss or colleague is showcasing a new $5,000 watch and wants your reaction, shrug it off—politely—with a simple "Yeah, that's a nice watch." When you're at the company dinner, go ahead and order white wine with your steak if you want to. But be prepared. The Snob will be thrilled to remind you of your *faux pas.* Say thanks for the culinary tip—nicely—then explain that you get a terrible headache when you drink red wine.
- *Put your own house in order.* Why provide the Snob with fodder to trip you up? What messages are you sending to colleagues and superiors at work? Are you professional or unpolished? We hate to admit it, but there are some things to learn from the Snob: the sense of etiquette and

style; the participation in charity events, the ability to be comfortable and confident anywhere. Pay attention to your own dress, speech, and manners in the workplace. This does not mean you need to become a Snob. It does mean you should be well spoken and well turned out at the office. Don't make the Snob's job easier.

- *Be prepared for the Snob-noxious behavior.* Snobs act as if they tolerate people rather than appreciate them. And they like to get their way. When they don't, they sometimes sniff, sneer, huff, puff, and otherwise behave like spoiled brats. When they are having one of their fits, steer clear if you can, tell the Snob to lighten up if you dare, or pretend to feel their pain if you must.

Are You a Snob?
Bad habits can be unlearned.

- *Tone it down.* Keep your excellent taste to yourself. Don't rub it in. Reminding others that they are uncouth and that you are sophisticated will make you no friends or allies in the workplace.
- *Tolerate diversity.* We choose our friends. In most cases, we cannot choose our co-workers. A workplace is not a country club, or a church basement, or even a poker club or bowling league. It's not about being among "your people." It's about getting along with people. In every office there is a range of income and education levels, as well as diverse religious, racial, and ethnic groups. The Snob may never learn to celebrate diversity, but he should at least learn to tolerate it at the office.

- *Transform yourself from snobby to classy.* A person with class is elegant, poised, polished, polite, or charitable—or all of the above. Styles may change but *style* doesn't. The classy person is the bigshot who means it when he asks the receptionist how the children or grandchildren are doing.
- *Use your etiquette and style constructively.* Whether in the office, in business meetings, or at luncheons, you are poised and polished and can make a good impression. Try putting those skills to work for a good cause: volunteer, chair hospital fund-raisers, serve on the 5K run committee for breast cancer awareness, or get involved with the town's Little League.

Poisonous Blend

- *The Snob–Prima Donna.* These fraternal twins can make the workplace insufferable. By glorifying themselves, this combination has the power to make others feel utterly inferior, especially those who lack a clear sense of themselves and their worth. It takes a strong ego to survive around the likes of this hybrid.

THE COMPLAINER

You taught me language; and my profit on't is I know how to curse.

—CALIBAN, FROM SHAKESPEARE'S *THE TEMPEST*

It was Friday night and everybody was deciding where to go after the football game. "Oh, no, not pizza? [insert sigh here] I *hate* pizza!" *Everything* was said with a sigh. The homework assignment was too hard, or the desk was uncomfortable, or the walk was too far, or the date was a bore. Nothing was ever right.

The transition from high school to workplace was seamless. The Complainer had nothing good to say about anything or anyone then, and has nothing good to say about anything or anyone now. The Complainer wants you to explain, for the fifth time, why the company uses PCs instead of Macs. He thinks the vacation policy is stupid. "No way, can't be done" is his deadpan response to any new idea. The Complainer hates meetings, and everybody knows it.

It's 4:00 P.M. and the weekly staff meeting has just begun. The

Complainer has already asked when the meeting will end as he *must* leave by 4:45 to avoid the traffic.

It's 4:05 and the first agenda item, creating needed office space, is being discussed. The Complainer thinks the space allocated is already too small and can't conceive how to expand existing walls and footage to accommodate six additional work stations.

It's now 4:15. Agenda item number two: encouraging employees to attend two training seminars a year. The Complainer states that training is a waste of the employee's time and the company's money. "Furthermore," he says, "employees should be screened more carefully. They ought to possess the skills necessary to do their jobs when they're hired."

It's 4:30. Agenda item number four: approval of the communication plan. The Complainer's vote is—you guessed it—against the plan. "It's reactive, not proactive; it's defensive and wimpy," proclaims the Complainer.

Oh, God, please, the rest of us are thinking, *is it 4:45 yet?*

Indeed, the Complainer is very, very tiresome.

The Complainer's Communication Style

- Complainers do not often draw on sources of power like title, expertise, physical presence, or personality. They consider their source of power to be their skepticism of all sources of power.
- Negative people usually have negative communication styles. Posture is sloped. The handshake is weak or indifferent. They are physically withdrawn or defensive. The scowl, sneer, and look of boredom are more frequent facial expressions than the confident smile.

- The Complainer's use of negative language is so pervasive it's almost comical. A lack of energy and spark is pervasive in her voice. Ask another type how they're doing and you're likely to hear, "I'm great, thanks for asking!" Ask the Complainer and you're likely to get an answer like, "Things aren't so bad" or "I suppose things could be worse." Or you'll hear their latest gripe.
- The Complainer sees the world in black and white, and his language will skew heavily to the negative.

If Your Boss or Colleague Is a Complainer

- *Stay positive.* This is essential when you communicate with the Complainer, whether it's in person or in writing. The Complainer is always looking for an enabler, a comrade in negativity. Don't let him bring you down.
- *Solicit solutions.* When the Complainer is on a rant, ask what should be done to solve the problem. Encourage the Complainer colleague to talk to the cafeteria manager about the fresh-squeezed orange juice problem. Or offer to do so for the Complainer boss. Challenge the Complainer colleague to formulate and present to the boss an alternative vacation policy at the next staff meeting. The Complainer's worst nightmare is having nothing to complain about. And it's *your* worst nightmare to let him gripe endlessly without action or change.
- *When all else fails, marginalize.* Complainers rarely rise to senior positions. Because they are negative, they don't often get promoted. Because they don't get promoted, they are negative. It's a vicious cycle. They are usually

stuck in the middle or at the bottom of organizations. Tolerate them if you must, and avoid them if you can.

Are You a Complainer?

Bad habits can be unlearned.

- *Force yourself to say one positive thing a day.* Walk before you run. You won't lose your negative habits overnight. Start by finding something nice to say—in person or in writing. Or say nothing at all. Expressing doubts doesn't mean you're a negative, complaining person, but if that's *all* you do, you're going to keep that reputation. If you're always the one complaining, your co-workers will sit back and let you do so. You, not they, will keep the reputation of being a wet blanket, a party pooper. Turn the tables and change your image by being positive.
- *If you must criticize, use positive language and propose a solution.* *How* you say it is as important as what you say. As an exercise, try to flip every complaint into a positively worded statement. For example, "I'm so sick of three-hour meetings" becomes "I'd like to propose that our meetings now have a one-hour limit. If we had an agenda for meetings and assigned time limits to topics, we could accomplish in one hour what currently takes three. Do you agree?"
- *Take responsibility for your happiness.* If you hate your job, your company, your career, your life, or anything else, stop complaining and start fixing the problem. You'll be happier . . . and a lot easier to work with.

Poisonous Blend

- *The Complainer–Gossip*. The worst of two big-mouth types. The Complainer can't find anything good to say about anything or anyone, and the Gossip can't wait to let everyone else know it.

THE PRIMA DONNA

To love oneself is the beginning of a lifelong romance.

—OSCAR WILDE

"My mom wrote me a note to get out of class. You want to go to the mall?" The Prima Donna demanded and got special treatment. If *you* flunked, you got an F. The star athlete, on the other hand, got a passing grade from the teacher despite a dismal academic performance. The class beauty could convince admirers to write the needed history paper free of charge just for the privilege of being appreciated and a getting a hello in the hallway. The silver-tongued devil could talk his way out of anything: missing home-work, disciplinary action, even poor test scores.

The most frustrating thing about Prima Donnas is that often we really liked them and wanted to be their friend. In our enthu-siasm to get some of their "star rub-off" we ended up helping them get away with whatever they wanted to, kicking ourselves the whole way.

The Prima Donna dazzled everyone on the interview and arrived the first day of work bursting with confidence, enthusiasm, and ideas—*big* ideas. The charismatic Prima Donna declared that everything from that day forward would be different. And others not only believed it, they were happy to be conscripted.

The Prima Donna was involved in only the biggest and most important projects. Everything was urgent and critically important. Behold the Prima Donna: Talking on her cell phone on the way to the elevator, or tossing a really huge idea on the table for everyone to fall in love with at the weekly staff meeting. When the Prima Donna finally left the company seven months later, everyone agreed she was dazzling and talented . . . but no one was quite sure what she actually *did*. Tending to details is not part of the Prima Donna's repertoire.

While the less-talented Prima Donna sailed through high school without too many consequences, things can, and usually do, get stickier in the workplace. Talking one's way into a job and doing it are different skills. Passing the buck, stealing credit, complaining, and undermining workplace morale eventually catch up with the Prima Donna.

The Prima Donna is to the workplace what charcoal lighter fluid is to the barbecue pit: The flame is instant and intense . . . then frequently evaporates into thin air.

On the flip side: the phenomena of genuinely gifted Prima Donnas, often indulged from an early age. They often soar to the top without having to do the grunt work. They've either been told by others or are happy to tell you that they are smarter than everyone else. And make no mistake about it: they *are* talented. They *are* smart. They are all big ideas, big bluster, and big results—and they believe you exist to serve them.

The Prima Donna's Communication Style

- This type has remarkable written, spoken, and interpersonal communications skills.
- The Prima Donna has one communications objective: helping the world understand how lucky it is to have her around. The craftiest Prima Donnas convince you to make them look good. Prima Donnas are expert flatterers, and know instinctively how to exploit their image—and your vulnerabilities—to their advantage.
- Prima Donnas communicate *upward*. They are vaguely interested in peer-level colleagues, and frequently ignore subordinates altogether.
- They are uncomfortable and off balance with colleagues or subordinates they can't impress. Even more threatening is the rival who is equal or superior in talent level. When two or more Prima Donnas square off in the workplace, it is usually to the demise of one of them.

If Your Boss or Colleague Is a Prima Donna

- *Talk business, not flattery.* Flattery, praise, recognition, and credit are oxygen for the Prima Donna. Often, you control the supply. Administer it judiciously to the Prima Donna boss, and even more judiciously to Prima Donna peers and subordinates.
- *Widen your circle of support.* The Prima Donna is number one. You are a distant number two. If you do choose to align yourself with your Prima Donna boss or col-

league, make a lot of allies, as you may find yourself in a tough spot if the Prima Donna leaves.

- *Escape!* Over time, Prima Donna bosses drive talented people away. The people who remain are often weak and fawning. The projects and departments they are affiliated with often rot slowly from the inside. In the long term, you're better off finding a new opportunity.

Are You a Prima Donna?

Bad habits can be unlearned.

- *Command respect; don't demand it.* The rewards are even richer when you apply your considerable charisma and talent to inspire rather than sublimate people. Earn the praise and recognition you crave.
- *Share the spotlight.* This is the sincere way to inspire others, particularly if you are a boss. The power you acquire at the expense of others is small potatoes compared to the power you will be given by sharing some of the wealth. It has been said many times and many ways, but it's true: you get a lot more by giving.
- *Get your hands dirty.* Keeping the plum assignments for yourself while tossing crumbs to others generates resentment. Pitch in and help others with low-glamour assignments.
- *Don't just look to the top of the pyramid.* In order to be effective and earn respect throughout your company, cultivate relationships at all levels of the hierarchy. Remember that anyone you snub, take credit from, or run

over today could end up being your boss tomorrow. As the cliché goes, what goes around comes around.

Poisonous Blend

- *The Prima Donna–Class President.* When these types mix, glory seeking and charisma come together, and it can be miserable for everyone who has to live in this person's orbit. The Prima Donna–Class President uses innate charm and a sense of entitlement to capture the stage, then never, ever leaves. This is an outsized ego run amok.

THE GOSSIP

If you can't say anything good about someone, sit right here by me.

—ALICE ROOSEVELT LONGWORTH

"Ohmygod! You're not going to believe what I heard!" This student, breathless with excitement, was always first with breaking news about breakups, dating debacles, social slights, unrequited loves, and all forms of catastrophe, large and small. The Gossip was obsessed with the triumphs and humiliations of others, the more personal, the better. The Gossip's fascination with others was usually couched as praise ("Wow, Susan must have more going for her than I gave her credit for. Did you know she's going to the prom with Luke?"), or concern ("Poor Tony, he's been a disaster since Joan dumped him for Kevin!"). The less clever Gossips were simply nasty ("Did you hear Maria's dad lost everything in the stock market and they have to move to a smaller house?").

Later in life, at the office, Gossips are the ones who are happy to discuss the boss's divorce, the winners and losers in the departmental reorganization, and whether the two managers you suspect are sleeping together really are. In fact, on the commute to work, you can count on the office Gossip to be on his cell phone with a colleague or, in a pinch, anyone who'll listen.

"Just wait until you hear what I overheard working late last night," the Gossip teases. "It's probably going to be announced in a couple of weeks."

"What are you talking about?" queries the person on the other end of the cell phone, sufficiently sucked into the Gossip's whirlwind.

"It's going to affect the whole sales organization!"

"No! What are you talking about?"

In total command, the Gossip continues. "There's going to be a total reorg. The VP is getting the boot—and I can just guess why. There's going to be a lot of infighting for that job and maybe some other heads are going to fall."

An audible pause. Then, "No . . . you've got to be kidding!"

"Uh-unh. I kid you not. More later."

Clearly, for the Gossip, the workplace is as much about intrigue as it is about product.

The Gossip's Communication Style

- The Gossip cannot rely on title, expertise, physical presence, or personality to win over the audience. His communications currency is *information*.
- They have amazing Jekyll-and-Hyde communication style. When extracting information, they are all empathy and all ears. They will crawl on their bellies through the slimiest details of others' lives in search of a gold nugget. Once they strike gold, they strut and swagger like mil-

lionaires as they broadcast the salacious news to co-workers.

- Gossips are almost always gifted speakers and engaging storytellers. Many also write well, including on e-mail.
- They are not at their best in large groups. If forced, they can talk to a group at a meeting, but they much prefer to be one-on-one at lunch, listening very, very carefully as you reveal more than you should.

If Your Boss or Colleague Is a Gossip

- *Button your lip.* Once the Gossip starts tempting you into a discussion about sensitive information, the easiest thing to do is simply refuse to play by saying, "That subject is off limits for me" or "I'm not comfortable talking about that."
- *Turn the tables.* If you can't walk away instantly (the Gossip may be your boss), try to say nothing and deftly turn the tables. You ask the questions. Most Gossips gossip out of insecurity. They are often terrified that people will really get to know them. They are busy hiding behind other people's lives. Flush the Gossip out. Make her answer personal questions about *her* career objectives, love interests, friends, enemies at work, and so on. This levels the playing field fast.
- *If you must play, play nice.* If you must gossip, strictly adhere to the *New York Times* rule: Never say or commit anything to paper that you would not like to see reprinted on the front page of the *New York Times*, attributed to you.

Are You a Gossip?

Bad habits can be unlearned.

- *Stop gossiping.* Why? Because it undermines your credibility. People will know you for "soft" information, even if it is sometimes useful or entertaining. You'll get to the top faster if you get famous for communicating ideas about work instead of being infamous for dishing dirt.
- *Confidentiality is king.* Demonstrate that you can be trusted with confidential information. If senior management doesn't believe you can keep a secret, you are less likely to be trusted or promoted. Interestingly, the power and inside information you enjoy now by gossiping will double when people find out they can tell you confidential news and you won't repeat it.
- *Redeploy your skill.* You have proven that you can build relationships. You have a terrific network of contacts, cronies, and comrades. Leverage your considerable social talents to build alliances, and you can transform yourself from an inveterate gossip to a skilled office politician.

Poisonous Blend

- *The Gossip–Know-it-all.* For the sake of personal advancement, the Gossip–Know-it-all talks about others, and does so with an attitude. This type not only spreads information but it is pejorative as well. Gossip–Know-it-alls malign reputations and alienate people with their superior attitude, crippling careers—their own and others'—along the way.

THE BROWN-NOSER

I suppose flattery hurts no one, that is, if he doesn't inhale.
—ADLAI STEVENSON

Remember the first time the Brown-noser came to your house for dinner? Your mother was told that she made the best chicken the Brown-noser *ever* tasted. "You should open a restaurant. I mean it, you really should!" said the Brown-noser. Five minutes later, in response to your dad's question about college and future job plans, the Brown-noser said a career in hospital administration sounded intriguing. Coincidentally, your dad was a hospital administrator.

Flattery: It's the oldest trick in the book. And on most people, it works. Who doesn't like to be told that their suggestion was brilliant, that they are the only one who can complete a task the right way? In fact, who doesn't like being told something as simple and seemingly benign as "You look great. Have you lost some weight?"

So what's the harm? Well, there's a fine line between flattery and insincerity. And then there's the matter of motive. There are two kinds of Brown-nosers in the workplace: those who do harm to themselves and those who do harm to others. The benign Brown-nosers are insecure and merely annoying; we are embarrassed for them and their shamelessness. Remember Eddie Haskell from *Leave It to Beaver* and his obsessive politeness and endless, phony praise to Mr. and Mrs. Cleaver? The more dangerous Brown-nosers, on the other hand, are operators with a hidden agenda. They use people for their own purposes. Watch your back! All grown up now, the Brown-noser's conversation hasn't changed much.

When the boss says the budget has to be reconciled and turned in at the end of business tomorrow and laments not knowing how it will ever get done in time, the fawning schemer and false friend, masquerading as a patron, says, "Give me that!" in a perfectly calibrated tone that's part scolding, part playful.

"You shouldn't be doing these stupid budgets. Budgets are for little people like me to handle. You should free yourself up to think about the big-picture stuff. I'll do the details. Now go home, leave, get. Give yourself some time to breathe and freshen up before you have to be the center of attention at the Awards Dinner tonight," says the Brown-noser effusively.

The boss smiles, hands her the folder, and says, "You're still coming tonight, aren't you?"

"I wouldn't miss it for the world. What a great honor for you! And don't worry. The budgets will be on your desk by three o'clock tomorrow afternoon."

"You're a lifesaver," coos the boss, heading out the door.

Just what the Brown-noser wants the boss to think.

In the next minute, the Brown-noser leaves the boss's office and goes directly to the last cubicle on the left.

"Here you go, Kelly." The Brown-noser slaps the file on the desk.

"A. J. asked that you get the budget in shape. The numbers need to be verified and then returned to me. It's urgent. It's got to be done by noon tomorrow. You're the *only* one A. J. trusts checking these numbers, you know. *Me?* Oh. I've got to go to this stupid thing tonight—the Pacesetters Awards Dinner." Heavy sigh and concomitant rolling of the eyes. "You know A. J."

Fuming inwardly, Kelly reboots her computer and settles in for a long night.

The Brown-noser's Communication Style

- The Brown-noser's source of power is title, physical presence, and personality—*yours*. Brown-nosers don't know how to behave when they're not flattering you. In fact, they are usually hiding from themselves and you in one way or another and don't want to be "discovered."
- Brown-nosers often write and speak well. Or, at least they *seem* to. When someone defers to you and flatters you in e-mails, in meetings, or over the telephone, what they say is a lot more memorable than how they say it.
- Brown-nosers, particularly the sneaky ones, do what they do to acquire power. Once they get it, they often abuse it. (They have been masking their contempt for you the whole time they were sucking up to you. Now it's payback time.)
- Winston Churchill defined an appeaser as someone who feeds a crocodile—hoping it will eat him last. The

Brown-noser is the ultimate appeaser, flattering you, laughing at your jokes, and catering to your every whim in the hopes you'll keep him around.

If Your Boss or Colleague Is a Brown-noser

- *Don't be seduced by the flattery.* Don't let all the Brown-noser's hot air cloud your judgment. Odds are, you are not as attractive, intelligent, witty, stylish, or insightful as you are being told. If it's your boss who's being seduced by this faker, just stand back, get out of the way, and do the best work you can while making sure that the boss recognizes you for your work.
- *Button your lip.* Don't reveal personal information to the Brown-noser. The best Brown-nosers will cultivate your trust, extracting confidential information about your personal life or professional matters. Then they use it to *their* advantage. Don't provide kindling for their fire. Your candor may come back to haunt you.
- *Turn the tables.* By making you feel great, the Brown-noser assumes you'll never question his skills . . . or motives. Interrogate him. Brown-nosers love to talk about you, but don't like to reveal who they are. Sure, some of them may chatter on about their own personal lives, but listen carefully and you'll discover they are not telling you much. So when you're finished quizzing him about his favorite restaurants and TV shows, start asking more penetrating personal questions. Watch the Brown-noser squirm.

Are You a Brown-noser?
Bad habits can be unlearned.

- *Flatter selectively.* Remember the law of supply and de-mand. When the government prints too much money, the value of the dollar is cheapened. When you put too many compliments in circulation, the same thing hap-pens. Flattery is not the same as sincerity, and the people around you can tell the difference.
- *Work on your own credentials.* It takes brains and talent to be an effective flatterer, talker, and listener. Imagine if you redeployed that energy into being taken seriously as a colleague rather than dismissed as a sycophant. Start trusting yourself.
- *Develop confidence.* If you don't know how to acquire power or credibility or prestige on your own, you can learn. The long-term solution isn't to get it through oth-ers, though many in the workplace do attach themselves to the coattails of bosses or colleagues. But by doing so, they never learn to stand on their own merits.

Poisonous Blend

- *The Brown-noser–Gossip.* This nasty hybrid flatters you, se-cures your trust, then sells you out. Just like your high school friend who gently coaxed you into revealing your lustful dreams about your favorite teacher and professed utmost compassion and understanding—only to tell the whole class by the time Homeroom began the next day. That same betrayal occurs daily in offices everywhere. Beware.

THE KNOW-IT-ALL

Questioning is not a mode of conversation among gentlemen. It is assuming a superiority.

—SAMUEL JOHNSON

The time: your junior year. *The place*: English class. *The occasion*: the Know-it-all is pontificating again. Wrestling for control with your teacher—"Ms. Bor, Shakespeare was *not*, beyond all reasonable doubt, the author of all the works attributed to him. There is significant research to suggest he may very well have plagiarized the work of an Italian playwright or that Francis Bacon authored the plays that bear Shakespeare's name." Ah, yes, Know-it-alls let everyone within earshot know they know it all. They are at the head of the class in one-upsman ship. They live to catch others making a mistake. And whenever they raised their hands in class to speak, the rest of us rolled our eyes because we knew they were always challenging the teacher's authority and exerting their own.

Some years later: A new reporter has been assigned to cowrite a story with the Know-it-all, who works as an investigative reporter for the *Daily Express*. The Know-it-all has some hierarchy to establish.

"How long have you been a journalist?" asks the Know-it-all.

"This is my first newspaper job," says the fledgling reporter.

"Oh."

"I think I'm a pretty decent writer, though," says the new reporter. "I published a novel while I was still in college. After I graduated from Princeton, I worked at the White House, where I wrote speeches for the president. After that, I published an essay in *Forbes*."

"I see. But you've never written for a newspaper, then. Is that right?"

"That's right," says the new reporter.

"Well, it's quite different, our business—the news business. We are insistent that language be used properly. We're much tougher and more exacting than book publishers and politicians, I'm afraid. For example, I cringe when I see a sentence that reads, 'Over three hundred people attended the rally.' Do you know what's wrong with that sentence?"

Before the new hire has a chance to respond to the question, the Know-it-all helpfully answers. "The word 'over' refers to spatial relationships, as in 'The plane flew over Baltimore.' Whereas the words 'more than' signify quantity. Hence, the correct way to write the sentence is, 'More than three hundred people attended the rally.' "

"That's good to know," says the reporter.

"When you worked in the White House, did they teach you about the misuse of *admit* and *confess*?"

"I'm afraid not."

"I suspected. Well, everyone wants to *confess* that they have a secret to tell. But one cannot confess unless one has been formally accused; in other words, when one volunteers information, that's an admission, not a confession," says the Know-it-all.

"That's great to know," says the new reporter.

"And another common mistake: The speaker *implies*, and the hearer *infers*. Do you—"

"Oh, yes, I know about that rule," chirps the reporter. "In fact, I'm drawing an inference right now as you speak. . . ."

Indeed, in the workplace, Know-it-alls always have something to say because they like having the last word, letting others know how much *they* know. Or letting us believe they know more than they actually do. They are constantly seeking our endorsement, our admiration for all they know.

The Know-it-all's Communication Style

- Know-it-alls believe in themselves. They are confident that they are right and knowledgeable. And that confidence in their knowledge is their source of power. (It is also the source of irritation to people around them.)
- They are not shy about speaking up and being heard. In fact, they like the power that holding court gives them.
- Know-it-alls *may* know a lot, but they often don't know how to say it well. Their desire to talk and to be right is greater than their desire to be heard. If a colleague has suggested there are five strategies that will work, a Know-it-all will come up with a sixth, saying blatantly that others have overlooked the obvious.
- The Know-it-all's tone and language are judgmental, even condescending. And the Know-it-all's body lan-

guage mirrors disapproval. Arms are often crossed over the chest, the body is stiff, even a bit turned away from the person in charge. Indeed, the Know-it-all has trouble giving up authority or having colleagues look to another for it.

If Your Boss or Colleague Is a Know-it-all

- *Invite others to talk.* Know-it-alls thrive on keeping control by talking, by questioning, by putting out a banana peel and waiting for someone to slip on it so *they* look smarter. When the Know-it-all colleague keeps interrupting with questions or information, try saying, "I appreciate your contributions. Thank you. Now let's hear what others have to say."
- *Beat Know-it-alls at their own game.* Anticipate the Know-it-all's need to control and to feel superior. If you expect her to behave a certain way, you can prepare your comments ahead of time. For example, when you finish saying something, you can add, "I'm sure Janet would like to add some thoughts to what's just been discussed." Or, "Before I share my ideas with you, let's hear from Janet." By doing this you acknowledge the Know-it-all's need for power, and you show both her and your other colleagues that you are big enough to handle it.
- *Make the Know-it-all an ally rather than an adversary.* As annoying as Know-it-alls can be, their attention to picayune detail can be valuable. Try to engage her privately, letting her know you value her input but want to allow others a chance to participate. If that one-on-one talk

gets you nowhere, you're left to deal with the situation publicly. You can make statements such as, "For the sake of time, I'd like to take your questions after the meeting, in private," or "Thank you for that clarification," then quickly move on to someone else.

Are You a Know-it-all?

Bad habits can be unlearned.

- *Stop nitpicking.* At least in public. Let your colleague save face. Approach the person privately if you disagree or have another point to add. While both A Students and Know-it-alls share a penchant for getting things right, A Students ferociously attend to details in their search for excellence and personal perfection. Know-it-alls, on the other hand, nitpick to simply correct and show off their superiority. For the former it is a lifelong journey to find the Holy Grail; for the latter it is primarily a power trip.
- *Learn tact.* Your comments and assertions will be better received if they are delivered with consideration and care. Watch your tone of voice and keep from sounding as if you are delivering a lecture to inferiors or wrongdoers. Find ways to add your opinion without discounting others'. For example, instead of saying, "That's wrong," why not try, "Another way to look at it is . . ." or, "Have you considered . . ."
- *Give others a chance to contribute.* Giving up the floor in meetings allows others to be more engaged—and will also reflect better on you. Others will stop seeing and hearing you as the "yes, but" person and start seeing you

as a person who values what other people think and know.

- *Produce more output with less input.* Work more quietly and produce more. Based on your increased productivity, others will begin to give you the endorsement you crave.

Poisonous Blend

- *Know-it-all–A Student.* This type has all the answers and won't shut up. To make him even more insufferable, he often has the *right* answers.

THE BULLY

*There is no arguing with Johnson; for when his pistol misses
fire, he knocks you down with the butt end of it.*

—OLIVER GOLDSMITH

If you were smart, strong, popular, or good looking in high school,
odds are you and the Bully never crossed paths. The Bully knew
better than to tangle with *you*. The Bully is *not* an equal-
opportunity offender. Bullies don't like to pick on people their own
size. The Bully only feels big when others feel small.

Every morning at 7:55 you and the Bully step on the elevator
at the same time. While you continue to say "Good Morning"
every day, you have absolutely no expectations that your greeting
will be acknowledged or returned; it never has been, not once. The
Bully is several levels higher than you in the company, figuratively
and literally. You say, "Excuse me," and push eight. The Bully plows
through the crowd and pushes fourteen. The Bully parks in the
center of the elevator and doesn't budge; everyone must climb
over, under, or around to get in or out.

Just before the doors open on the eighth floor, the Bully grunts.

You are shocked. He addresses you by name. You are doubly shocked.

"Did you hear about the layoffs that are coming, Juergens? Wonder if you'll survive?" He is still grinning diabolically as the elevator doors squeeze shut.

At some point in our careers, each of us has worked for or with a Bully. They are almost always the same, whether they are restaurant managers, office supervisors, or executive vice presidents at multinational corporations. Early on in their careers, Bullies didn't have power. They coveted it, finally got it, and are determined to never, ever lose it. Bullies are paranoid and insecure. They prey on the weaker and smaller, bludgeoning subordinates and co-workers over the head with words instead of fists. With their words they scream, spook, frighten, intimidate, and belittle . . . *but only if you let them.*

The Bully's Communication Style

- Everything is a win-lose scenario. The Bully hates to negotiate. Negotiation requires nuance and skill, which the Bully usually doesn't have.
- This type is usually telling everyone else what to do.
- Personal presence is strong, forceful, charismatic, and pushy.
- Posture, facial expressions, and vocal vitality are animated, energetic.
- The Bully is constantly flexing physical, verbal, and intellectual muscle. It's all about your sublimation. You start a sentence, the Bully hijacks the conversation. You introduce an idea at the meeting, the Bully has a bigger

one . . . and wants everyone in the room to know it. Whether the Bully is six feet six and 275 pounds or five feet two and 120 pounds, physical swaggering and elbowing are used to advantage.

- Some Bullies, especially the Bully boss, are masterful at using silence as a tactic. You say something to them, and they refuse to react. For example, they never reply to the e-mail message you sent. Phone calls are ignored.
- Bullies take command. They will speak softly, loudly, charmingly, boldly—any way that enables them to capture and control the conversation.

If Your Boss or Colleague Is a Bully

- *Don't be afraid.* Even if the Bully is your boss, take a deep breath and know that when he screams and shouts, it's only words he's swinging around like a baseball bat. The Bully can't *really* hurt you. Just smile and let the Bully rant. Remember, the power Bullies have over you is the power you give them.
- *Stand your ground.* Bullies are notorious cowards, terrorizing others to mask their own insecurities. The Wizard of Oz scared the daylights out of everyone—until a pipsqueak dog and teenage girl took him on. Once the curtain was pulled back—figuratively and literally—his tough-guy act was over. Remember, too, that while King Saul thought Goliath was too big to fight, little David thought Goliath was too big to miss. And he was right.
- *Parent the Bully.* Bullies almost always have terrible manners. They are inconsiderate. They don't listen. They cut

in. They talk fast. Talk to the Bully as though you were a parent, or a patient teacher. Speak slowly. "Please, if you'll just let me finish my sentence . . ." or "John was making an important point and I would like to hear what he has to say." This technique is particularly effective in group settings.

- *Don't let him bully you on paper, either.* Bullies like to push and shove and throw their weight around, even on paper. There are two kinds of paper Bullies. First is the thug who flexes capital letters and exclamation points like muscles. His message is delivered in a barking, demanding, blunt, rude tone. Whisper—without surrendering—when you reply to this type. The contrast between your measured tone and objectivity and his shouting will be obvious to you (and the people you copy on your reply). More intimidating, but similarly infuriating, is the second type of Bully, the fencer who slices away at you with one elegantly written sentence after another. Be careful: He's setting a trap. He's hoping *you* will get mad and inarticulate and reply in all capital letters. Instead, take a deep breath, then carefully craft a reply in a voice that is quiet and low. Remember, this is the same Bully you dealt with before—he's simply wearing a silk suit.

Are You a Bully?
Bad habits can be unlearned.

- *Pick on someone your own size.* On second thought, stop picking on people—period. Redeploy your energy and learn to get what you want from others by enticing them with carrots rather than beating them with sticks.

- *Slow down.* If you run over people like a freight train you will inevitably get derailed. On the other hand, if you slow down and give people a chance to get on board, the journey will be smoother and more enjoyable for everyone.

- *Become an active listener.* Not all Bullies are inherently mean. Some are just unknowingly pushy or rude, especially in conversation. Make your point, then stop. Enforce personal silence. Give the other person a chance to talk. Monologues are for Shakespearean actors.

- *Keep your passion in check.* Some Bullies bully unintentionally. They have so much enthusiasm, conviction, or determination that they run roughshod over everyone. If you're one of these people you may be intimidating everyone around you without even realizing it. Pay attention to how you're coming across. Give folks a chance to catch up.

Poisonous Blend

- *The Bully–Go-getter.* Muscle and blind ambition are a brutal combination. This type definitely leaves its mark on the world, in the form of notorious political dictators and insufferable Hollywood agents.

THE CHEATER

*The world is divided into people who do things and people
who get the credit. Try, if you can, to belong to the first
class. There's far less competition.*
        —DWIGHT MORROW, IN A LETTER TO HIS SON

There you were sophomore year, slumped at your desk in homeroom. You knew exactly what was coming when the Cheater slid
into the seat beside you and started his con. "Hey, did you do the
chemistry assignment? Did you get stumped on number seven like
I did?" The Cheater was at it again, pretending this was only about
number seven. "Say, any chance I could see what you did with it?
Oh, thanks." The Cheater chatted casually while peeking at your
number seven—and devoured numbers one through six, and numbers eight through twenty, too, making a mental photocopy of your
assignment. "Well, what do you know? It turns out your answer is
not much different than mine," he lied.

Months later, during finals, when word got out that someone
had stolen the answers to the chemistry exam from a locked file
cabinet in the main office, you just *knew* who did it. Of course,
the Cheater didn't get caught.

They rarely get caught as adults, either. With no compunction about lying on his résumé about background, education, and professional accomplishments, the Cheater will always find somebody who will hire him.

On the job, the Cheater, ever the wolf in sheep's clothing, continues the sting he started in school. In adulthood, his smoke-and-mirrors act is more sophisticated.

"I have an idea I want to run by you," says a co-worker.

"Shoot," says the Cheater.

The co-worker, brimming with enthusiasm, unveils a plan to reduce shipping costs company-wide by twenty-five percent.

The Cheater is half listening to the presentation. He is bored and unimpressed (or pretends to be). When the pitch is over, the Cheater reacts with a sigh and a few carefully chosen words.

"There are a hundred reasons why your plan won't work. But do me a favor anyway. Send me an e-mail with a summary, and I'll try to work some of the bugs out for you."

The lamb is grateful for the wolf's interest. The co-worker sends the e-mail to the Cheater.

An hour later, the Cheater sends an e-mail to the top boss. "Subject: How to Reduce Shipping Costs by 25%."

The first line of the e-mail: "Lately I've been wracking my brain trying to figure out ways to save this company money, and I think I'm onto something. . . ."

Be careful, because the Cheater may steal a lot more than your thunder. Tragically, the damage caused by this type is often commensurate with the Cheater's audacity. Beware the Cheater whose posturing is polished, upright, and sincere. This type is often the perpetrator of the *really* big lie. This is the bamboozler who gets you to invest in a "sure thing" hedge fund, then mysteriously disappears with your and everyone else's money in hand.

The Cheater's Communication Style

- The Cheater's innate insecurity governs his communication style. This type lacks the confidence and the skills to shine alone. With diminished personal power, the Cheater, like a vampire, feeds off others to keep himself going.
- Cheaters are master communicators. Cheaters, particularly the credit stealers, are notoriously sly with language. Your idea morphs into theirs. Everything they say is arranged to give them maximum credit with minimum accountability. Every claim has an escape hatch they can trigger if someone backs them into a corner.
- Cheaters are charmers. They are smart enough not to deliberately antagonize colleagues who can furnish them with the answers.
- The Cheater is brash and overconfident. The Cheater is nervy, even bombastic at times. He is always selling the big idea—*yours!*

If Your Boss or Colleague Is a Cheater

- *Expose him.* Depending on your workplace, you might be able to tell someone in power about the Cheater's methods directly (the ideal situation) or you may need to be subtler. Because many Cheaters have an inflated opinion of their own skills and expertise, it is often useful (and fun!) to find creative ways to have them "tested" in a public forum.

- *Expose yourself.* "Get caught" doing good work. The Cheater wants to keep you hidden under a rock. Come out from under it. Look for ways to make sure that the top bosses know it's you who's doing the work and generating the ideas.
- *Quit talking to him.* Your words, conversations, e-mails, and memoranda are the Cheater's oxygen. Deny him as much oxygen as you can, for as long as you can.

Are You a Cheater?
Bad habits can be unlearned.

- *Deploy communication skills constructively.* Cheaters with the gift for gab will be just as dazzling if they are selling their own work instead of someone else's.
- *Do your own homework.* There are examples of people who successfully lie, cheat, and scheme their way to the top. But these examples are rare—and these operators rarely last. Success is about competence and personality. The Cheater is already a charmer and is thus halfway there; now comes the work. Do it.
- *Collaborate.* The Cheater co-opts other people's ideas. The collaborator makes the team look great. Sharing credit is like sharing compliments: generally speaking, the more you give, the more you get.
- *Earn your colleagues' trust.* Offer a helping hand to others. Doing so will help reverse your negative image. Give

away an answer or two to a stumped colleague or team that is struggling to solve a problem. And let them take the credit for resolving it. They'll come to you again once they see that you've played fairly. Then you can share the rewards rather than hoard them.

Poisonous Blend

- *The Cheater–Brown-noser.* This type is dangerous indeed. Oily, underhanded, and remorseless, he or she will use words—and people—to personal advantage. The Cheater–Brown-noser is the Trojan horse of the workplace: attractive and smiling on the outside, but full of deceit within. Beware co-workers like this bearing gifts!

THE PLAYER

"What kind of idiot," she wondered, "lets her husband go
to Paris with a person like me."
—JONATHAN FRANZEN, *THE CORRECTIONS*

Every high school had them. They sat in the back of the room,
undressing classmates with a glance. Or they passed explicit notes
that did the same. Or there they were in the stairwell, backing a
prospect up against the wall. Many were immortalized in bathroom
stalls, their names and numbers etched on the wall by boasting
conquerors or disgruntled conquests.

Mastery of the Pythagorean theorem was not their thing. Academic performance took a backseat to backseat performance. It
was in animal magnetism that they earned their A's. Parents knew
instantly what this kid was about when they met the Player at the
homecoming game: the catlike moves, the clothes that fit just right
in all the right places, the eye contact that lasted a few seconds too
long.

Players are opportunists who choose—or allow themselves to
be chosen. Maybe his self-esteem needs refueling. Or she is bored

and looking for entertainment. Or perhaps it is simply hormones run amuck. Whatever the reason, the Player uses sex to manipulate others. And in the workplace, Players are keenly aware that sex and power can be closely intertwined.

Mr. Findlay, looking quizzical, sits at his desk. Ms. Rodgers, who reports to Mr. Findlay, pokes her head in the open office door.

"Is everything okay?"

"I just got the strangest call," he says.

She invites herself to sit down.

"From whom?"

"Some woman from the promotions department at the Glitz Hotel. They're opening a new spa and they offered me a complimentary massage tomorrow at noon."

"Lucky you," she says.

"So you think I should take it?"

"That's the wrong question," she says with a smile. "The real question is: Do you like being touched by strangers?"

He blushes. She pushes further.

"Doesn't Ellen give you massages at home once the kids are asleep?

She won't drop it. "You're not afraid, are you?"

The next day at noon he arrives at the Glitz Hotel. And, as instructed the day before, he knocks on the door of room 227. It opens. His jaw drops. Ms. Rodgers, wrapped in a terry cloth robe, asks if he'd like a glass of champagne before they get started.

The Player's Communication Style

- Players can be vulgar and uninhibited: Shock value is a popular tactic for the manipulator. Or their language can be soft and complimentary, flattering before the kill. Either way, when they talk, we listen.

- The Player's primary source of power comes from body language. Players communicate sex. They create a presence with their movements, their looks, their gestures. Watch the way they lower themselves into a seat or onto a sofa, crossing one leg over the other deliberately, slowly, gracefully. They hope you are watching, because all of this is for your benefit.

- Players talk most when they aren't even opening their mouth. When they do speak, they are likely to echo what their body has already spoken: that they are attractive, desirable, and willing. Often they will rely on well-worn lines to "close the deal."

- The Player's wardrobe showcases an attractive physique. This is not to say that everything a female Player wears is sexy or sleazy. Or that a male Player is clad in skin-tight pants. They simply understand how to wear clothing that highlights their best features and hides their flaws. They dress for sexual success.

If Your Boss or Colleague is a Player

- *Try befriending her.* The Player is often more embarrassing to herself than dangerous. Thus, the Player might need a friend who can hold a mirror up and show what others have been seeing. (This is more easily accomplished if the Player is a colleague.) The Player wants power and respect. Help her find it. A good friend can help the Player develop other skills. Does the Player write well?

Does the Player have a quick mind or a good sense of humor? Suggest that the Player sign up for seminars that will help develop new skills or enhance existing ones.

- *Avert your eyes.* If the Player refuses to downplay the sex, make it clear you cannot be seduced. Be "all business."
- *Stay out of it.* If the Player asks you to cover up for his whereabouts or asks to use your apartment the weekend you'll be out of town, take a deep breath and say "no." Don't let your good judgment wane because the Player's did.
- *Know your rights.* If the Player in your workplace is a predator and you are the prey, you may want to look into your rights and the company's harassment policies.

Are You a Player?
Bad habits can be unlearned.

- *Sell excellence, not sex appeal.* Begin to let your good work, not merely your attractiveness and sexual energy, carry you in the office. Instead of leading others on, lead a work effort to cut costs, win a new contract, or improve the product you sell.
- *Give yourself a makeover.* And we're talking about more than looks. Think about the messages your words, deeds, clothing, and body language are sending. Communicate good taste, style, and restraint. If you look and act as though you deserve respect, you'll get it.
- *Face reality.* What are the odds that the co-worker with whom you are having an illicit affair is going to leave

the spouse and kids for you? Instead of ruining innocent lives, get a new one yourself and start over.

Poisonous Blend

- *The Player–Go-getter.* Boldness abounds in this type who loves and courts danger, among other things, and, in the end, is willing to pay a very high price for sexual amusements. Sexual prowess and ambition fuse as this type sleeps its way to the top.

PART TWO

GETTING TO THE NEXT GRADE LEVEL: LESSONS ON ORGANIZATIONAL SURVIVAL

Stand firm in your refusal to remain conscious during algebra. In real life, I assure you, there is no such thing as algebra.

—FRAN LEBOWITZ

We hope you had fun reacquainting yourself with everyone in the class and discovering more about them and yourself. In this section of the book, we'll continue to examine how high school and work are strikingly alike, and discuss the skills required for success in either milieu.

In high school, we organize ourselves in cliques and clubs. In the workplace, we call these departments or business units, or teams. In high school, teachers reward students who do exactly what the teacher tells them to do. Ditto in the workplace. The boss plays the role of the teacher—just as faithfully as all the other members of the "class" we've described in Part One play their roles. In high school, misfits are excluded from the "cool" lunch tables. In business, misfits are excluded from golf outings, after-work drinks, and other extracurricular gatherings.

School isn't only about grades. Nor is work only about work.

Sure, in both places doing a good job contributes to success, but high school and work are not just about standing out. They are also about fitting in. About developing the ability to convince people that we are worth being liked, trusted, and included.

To get ahead, you've got to learn how to get along.

Successful people from seventeen to seventy-seven know how to get their point across, how to be taken seriously—with their behavior, their body language, their wardrobe, and their vocabulary. They persuade. They tell engaging stories. They are trustworthy and truthful. They know how to sound smart without sounding pompous. They make a good impression. They are memorable.

In short, they influence. And you can, too.

AUTHORITY

The organizational structures of high school and the corporate workplace are remarkably alike. Principals and CEOs are at the top of the organization chart. These authority figures can be aloof, iconic, formidable. In the middle of the organization are the teachers and bosses, who oversee the students and employees.

The Golden Rules in both organizations:

- If you're a student or employee, don't outshine the teacher or boss.
- If you're a teacher or boss, don't outshine the principal or CEO.

Any questions?

Your boss wants and expects humility and respect from you. Always remember this.

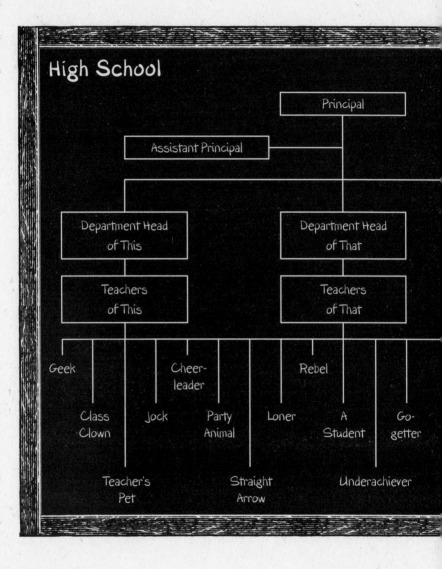

High School

Principal

Assistant Principal

Department Head of This

Department Head of That

Teachers of This

Teachers of That

Geek

Cheer-leader

Rebel

Class Clown

Jock

Party Animal

Loner

A Student

Go-getter

Teacher's Pet

Straight Arrow

Underachiever

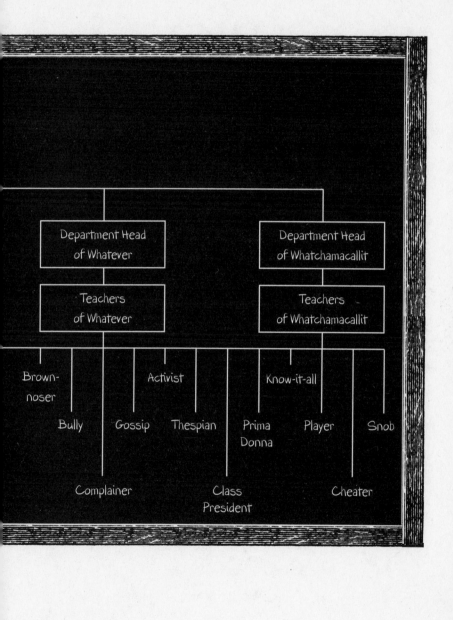

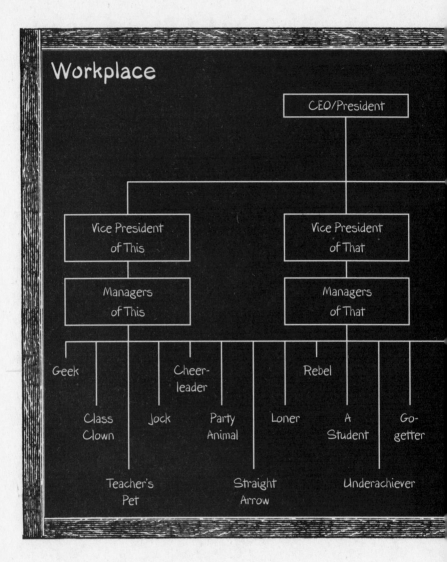

Workplace

CEO/President

Vice President of This

Vice President of That

Managers of This

Managers of That

Geek

Cheer-leader

Rebel

Class Clown

Jock

Party Animal

Loner

A Student

Go-getter

Teacher's Pet

Straight Arrow

Underachiever

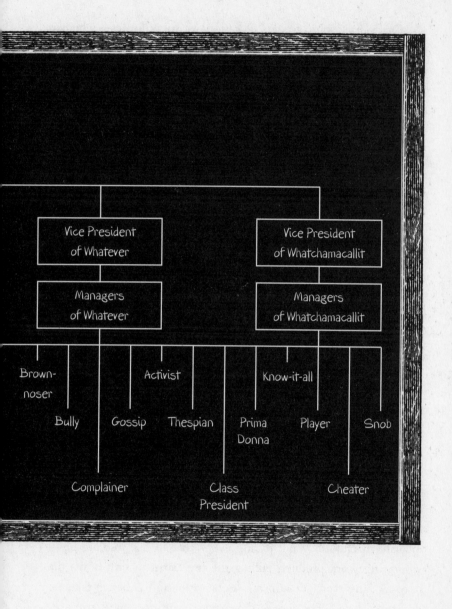

Of course, some forget. Occasionally, subordinates—whether students or employees—are smarter than their masters. They are foolish to make this known.

When the parties understand and accept their respective roles, teacher-student and boss-employee relationships can be incredibly rich for *both* parties.

Maybe you had a boss or teacher who changed your life; who inspired, mentored, and motivated you; who was secure and confident enough to talk to you like a peer or partner. You revered this teacher or boss for treating you like a person, not an underling. You would have stayed at school or the office until midnight if this teacher or boss needed your help on a project.

And then, of course, you probably also had the boss or teacher who made your life miserable; who ruled by intimidation and fear; who was petty; who treated you like a child. "Anyone who fails to write their essay in blue ink will receive an automatic F," sniped the English teacher before the exam. "Is black ink illegible?" you wondered. Ten years later you find the memo posted on the bulletin board, strikingly similar in tone: "Effective immediately, no one is permitted to go to the bathroom without first notifying the administrative assistant they will be leaving the work area."

When bosses treat employees like children, employees behave like children. One of the best illustrations of this sad truth is the strained relationship between management and organized labor in this country. Rank-and-file union members are often treated like children by management. In response to this slight, union workers retaliate in childish ways: testing every rule to the absolute limit, sabotaging work product, pulling the fire alarm to shut down the line. (As any teenager knows, *negative* attention is better than no attention at all.) The workers' behavior reinforces what management suspected all along: rank-and-file union members behave like children and therefore must be treated like children. It's a vicious circle.

The best high school teachers and workplace bosses bring you up to their level: when bosses treat adults like adults, employees behave like adults. This is the best way to encourage excellence and get results.

> **Lesson:** The recipe for harmony in the workplace is actually quite simple: people at all levels and ranks want and deserve to be treated with dignity and respect.

POPULARITY

Personality is the true coin of the realm—the magic stash—in high school and at work.

Of course, there are standards that must be met, lest you flunk out or get fired. Like passing quizzes and making widgets. Getting the work done and getting it done right are very important details, but they're still just details. Success as a teenager and in the workplace is largely about whether or not you are popular and likable. It's about your ability to fit in.

Good grades and good work don't guarantee success. "Get the basics right, and everything else will fall into line," our parents, teachers, and bosses tell us. It should be this way. But it isn't. If this prescription for success were true, there should be a direct correlation between a 4.0 grade point average in high school and college and becoming CEO of a major corporation, or a member of Congress, or a TV journalist. (Many successful people got B's and C's at state universities, not necessarily A's from Harvard.) They knew that they had to learn and pass courses, but they also knew that making friends—*who would become future contacts*—was equally important.

Plenty of valedictorians go on to success and satisfaction as adults, but just as many fizzle out like a sparkler on the Fourth of July once they get into the workplace. In fact, most people's work problems are not school related or job related; they are *people related*.

The teenagers on the margins who abused drugs or contemplated suicide or violence did not get into that spot solely because they were bad at algebra. Being misunderstood and ridiculed by other kids is devastating. In comparison, being bad at algebra is not. Likewise, when have you ever heard an adult say, "I quit my job. I just wasn't smart enough to get the job done." It's rare. People quit their jobs because "the culture wasn't right" or they had a "personality conflict" with the boss, or "others didn't show respect."

In order to survive and thrive, whether you are in high school or at work, you must get along with people. The first thing to remember is that likability is as important as talent. In high school, teachers found a way to punish the smart kids who were know-it-alls, showoffs, or simply arrogant brats. The insufferable honors student submitted a brilliant and insightful essay on the Argentine economy in the 1850s, only to be docked from A+ to A for a misspelling that got by the spellcheck, even after four proofreadings. The teacher was gleefully ready when the student contemptuously approached the desk after class to protest. On the other hand, the student who was atrocious at chemistry but humble and hardworking was tutored after class by a patient and supportive teacher.

In the workplace, colleagues and bosses will go to great lengths to publicize your failures if you are unlikable. But bosses can be incredibly generous with their time, and tend to mentor subordinates they like.

The talented and popular, in high school and at work, walk on water. The less talented but popular are coached. The talented but unpopular are undermined at every opportunity. The talentless and unpopular are in big, big trouble.

> **Lesson:** People who are competent and likable have an edge in organizations over those who are excellent at their jobs but unlikable.

CLIQUES

Remember Fonzie, the leather-clad character from the hit 1970s television show *Happy Days*? He was independent, a loner, a rebel, a tough guy, too cool for school. What you may *not* remember is that he wasn't part of the high school crowd because he wasn't a part of high school: he was a dropout. His isolation seemed cool at first, but it is worth noting that in the final season of the show he went back and earned his high school equivalency diploma after all. The ultimate outsider wanted to be part of a group—in this instance, the high school graduates' club.

No man or woman is an island . . . for long. People want and need to belong to groups. They want to have relationships with others. They want to connect. They want to find people who share their passions.

High schools cliques are infamous and blatant: the football players, the cheerleaders, the chess team, the debate squad, the blondes, the burnouts, the band geeks. In the workplace it's not quite as clear, but make no mistake, there are cliques everywhere. There's the golf clique, the marketing department, the field sales organization, or the gang that goes out for drinks every Friday afternoon, eats lunch together daily, or plays in the company softball league.

In high school, playing football or making the cheerleading squad is only partly about throwing blocks or doing the splits: it's also about *making the cut*. It's about exclusivity, status, belonging, about being granted admission. Indeed, in high school and at work, cliques can often be as much about who is kept *out* as who gets in. It isn't fair and it isn't nice. On occasion, it isn't even legal. But it is reality. And fair or not, we need networking and relationships to be successful in the workplace.

Happily, it is easier to break into a work clique than a high school one. Teens are notoriously cruel to each other. As adults, we are forced to behave more politely. Workplace decorum makes it harder to be rude. It is highly unlikely a colleague will say, "No, you can't join us for lunch," even though there are three unoccupied chairs at the table. In high school you may not have had the athletic skills to make the varsity team. In adulthood, the physical requirements are less demanding. If you want to break into the golf clique, you can learn to play golf and get good at it. Then invite someone to play. Even if you sense that the group isn't crazy about you, when a foursome is needed and it's well known you are a good player, the invitations will come.

If you want to gain entry into a workplace clique badly enough, there are ways in. If you absolutely cannot play softball, manufacture a reason to attend the games: put together a cheerleading squad, or offer to carry the coolers. Make silly trading cards with pictures of the players. In high school, people may have teased the student manager of the football or volleyball team who sat on the sidelines while the team played. But the manager was included in the team photo. And more important, the manager was invited to the party after the game.

Another option is to start your own club, so to speak. Why not kick off a book club at work? Or a cycling or stock club? Identify others who share your passions, expand the group, and occasionally invite people from other cliques. It is a great way to network with people in other parts of the department or company.

> **Lesson:** The door to almost any workplace clique will open if you have ingenuity and want in badly enough.

CHEATING

High school cheating is a lot like high school sex: Everybody *thinks* everybody else is doing it, when it fact, nearly everybody is *not*. Likewise, according to the U.S. Bureau of Labor Statistics there are 133.9 million Americans in the workforce. The overwhelming majority of them are decent, honest, hardworking people.

We take for granted how much we rely on trust until that trust is betrayed. Trust is the oil that keeps our social, political, and economic engines lubricated. Have elected officials in Washington ever really regained the credibility they enjoyed pre-Watergate? At the beginning of a new century, billion-dollar corporations that violated the public trust vaporize into nothing before our eyes. Their stock sells at $110 a share in April and by June the shares are traded at 23¢. See what we mean about trust and betrayal?

Let's bring this point even closer to home. Two kinds of Cheaters operate at school and at work:

- The Fraud, who is about *intent*.
- The Flawed, who is about *impact*.

The Fraud

This person is as subtle and smooth and slippery as an eel in Vaseline. The Fraud slithers up to you, charms you, disarms you, chats you up, then moves in for the kill. The Fraud is fundamentally crooked and, no doubt about it, intends to steal your ideas, your work, and your thunder.

The Fraud is the classic con artist, not just crooked but a crook. The homework thief who has no intention of ever doing homework again. The drug dealer in high school, or the scam artist who swindles the elderly out of their life's savings. Notoriously sly with language, Frauds can talk their way out of any problem.

The Flawed

This person is a more complex, and common, character. Is there a difference between cheating and being a cheater? Lying and being a liar? We are willing to bet that you have told a lie before, but that you don't consider yourself a liar. Just once, back in high school, did you ever take just a little teeny peek at someone else's work? Or did you ever stay home from work on a Friday or a Monday, pretending to be sick, just to extend your weekend? Or, perhaps you expensed a business dinner even though you skipped the meal?

The Fraud gets out of bed in the morning with the intention of ripping people off. But the Flawed doesn't mean to do any harm. When the chief financial officer at the global corporation is angling through traffic on her way to work, she does not laugh diabolically like Vincent Price, then proclaim, "Today I shall defraud every investor who ever sank a penny into my company!"

It's not that simple. It's never that simple with the Flawed. It starts out as a rationalization. The company has to report earnings. The company has to "make the numbers." The numbers-crunchers crunch and the next thing they're doing is "backing into the numbers." When that doesn't work, they "rob Peter to pay Paul." And so it goes.

We're not saying this is right. Clearly, it is not. What we're saying is that *this* is how human beings operate. Most ethical lapses don't happen the way they're portrayed in the movies. No stranger in a trench coat shows up unannounced at your workplace, flips open a briefcase stuffed with hundred-dollar bills, and makes you a crooked offer you can't refuse. Ethical slips are more subtle and usually start off small. The stock room delivered a few extra pads of paper so they wind up at home; a long distance call was made to friends from the office phone; an hour was spent on the Internet to order personal items during work hours while a report waited to be completed.

In the real world, it's usually not one massive mistake that brings you down . . . it's a thousand tiny ones. It's not one horrific ethics lapse—the dramatic death by swords or guns. For most people, it's death by a thousand paper cuts.

The best standard to apply at work is one we all apply at home. When you open up the refrigerator, occasionally you have to smell the food to make sure it's safe to swallow. So you raise the fish or the carton of milk up to your nose—and then you take a good long sniff. If it smells the *slightest* bit bad . . . well, you have your answer.

> **Lesson:** If you have to ask if it's ethical, fair, or right . . . then it probably isn't.

CONFORMITY

In high school, teens, parents, and teachers are, quite rightly, concerned about peer pressure. After all, it makes good kids do bad things like have unsafe sex, take drugs, or spend $109 on a pair of jeans.

Ironically, while high school students can be obsessed with conformity, they usually tolerate diversity better than adults. Corporations, on the other hand, usually claim to value diversity but are largely homogeneous and reward conformity.

Who dares to be the employee who, with freshly dyed cobalt blue hair, reports to work at the Wall Street brokerage house or the Main Street insurance agency? The workplace is incredibly good at communicating the boundaries of wardrobe, speech, behavior, humor, and values. In fact, most big companies have been so good at forcing everyone to look and behave alike that they now spend millions of dollars on diversity training seminars to deprogram employees and help them understand and celebrate their differences. Go figure.

Whether you are in high school or at work, you must figure out how to fit in. Pay close attention to what your company says and does when it comes to "values." The CEO and the senior management team tout company values like "imagination," "working smarter, not harder," "loyalty," "tenacity," "old-fashioned hard work," or "a balance between work and family." These are code words for what is expected of you if you expect to have success.

How fortunate if you find a company that shares your values. When you and the company are aligned, you will not feel like a conformist; you'll feel as though you are among your people; you'll have found a home away from home. But if the values of the organization are different from yours, the likely outcome of this match will be The Company: 1; You: 0. If you are a fighter, and have the stamina, you may want to challenge the culture head-on. Or you may try to adapt. For most people, though, it's an uphill battle. Most workers get frustrated and either give up or move on.

In short, it's often easier to switch than to fight. If you're smart, you'll do two things before your next job interview, whether it's in another department or at another company. First, make a list of the things that most excite and repel you about office culture. In other words, know yourself—your likes and dislikes. Second, ask managers and peers specific questions about the issues on your list.

If you ask questions, pay close attention, and listen closely to the answers you get about an organization's culture and norms, you'll know whether or not you can experience success there, or need to find a better fit.

Lesson: Though it values diversity, the organization expects you to embrace and conform to its values. If you can't or won't, you may be happier working somewhere else.

LOOKS

Remember telling your mom the *exact* sneakers, jacket, and jeans you *had* to have to complete your school outfit? And how good you felt when you strolled into school wearing them? You knew then that appearances matter; that wardrobe, looks, and personal style count; and that, rightly or wrongly, others do make initial judgments about you based on them. You looked through teen magazines, observed what the most popular kids at school were wearing, and decided which look would help you fit in rather than stick out.

You also knew—and maybe even felt—the stinging consequences of getting it wrong: embarrassment, ridicule, exclusion. There's little difference from yesterday's high school mockery in the parking lot to today's cruel whispers in the office about using too much fragrance, showing too much skin, or having too little taste. But you do have options: you can carry the style savvy you developed during high school straight to the boardroom. Or you can develop it now.

Of course, your appearance and the way you carry yourself matter—they always have. So let's start with the way you carry yourself into a room or meeting. If you didn't listen to your mother the first time, listen to us the second time: Stand up straight! You don't have to *be tall* to *seem tall*. Your height is as much a state of mind as a genetic gift. Take pride in yourself and comport yourself as if you do, and others will see what you are visualizing about yourself. And, while you're working on your physical presence at work, remember the value of eye contact and a smile to reassure others that you're confident and comfortable.

Next, to make a good appearance doesn't mean you need designer-label clothing. Let the good quality, good fit, and good taste of your attire speak for you. Look around your office. Chances are the people you admire at work, those who have succeeded, will have the appearance we're talking about here. To paraphrase Yogi Berra, "You can learn a lot by just looking."

Sure, some people, like Hollywood stars, get to wear pretty much anything they please. They make a career out of pushing the fashion envelope: it keeps them in the public eye. Keep in mind, though, that their appearance is their *job*. Many of them have personal trainers and do 11,000 sit-ups a day. They have their garments sewn on them before a big media event.

What works for them won't necessarily work for us mere mortals. For example, when Cher walks across the stage in rhinestone-studded purple spandex pants and an orange feather boa, it is a riveting sight. If your local bank teller is at all tempted to copy Cher's look, she would be wise to remember that a midsized bank in Toledo is a long, long way from a concert stage in Las Vegas.

Best to know the ground rules and add your own small flourish without being so overwhelming that people miss the real you.

Many image-minded companies like employees to wear company-logoed clothing; and some professions, or jobs, require a uniform be worn, be it a suit, scrubs, or scuba gear. Certainly, take direction about what to wear from what your company values and from what your job activities demand. But also reserve room for your personal style, within the boundaries of what's appropriate, especially in today's workplace where the style shifts back and forth from business casual to strictly business dress. If you have doubts about whether the outfit you've selected will be suitable at the office, chances are you ought to pick another. Let your clothing and your carriage be among your assets rather than your liabilities.

> **Lesson:** Style is not a substitute for substance. But your image is your opportunity to make a good first impression. And you rarely get a second chance to do so.

MANNERS

"Stop shoveling your food in!" "Don't talk with your mouth full!" "Use a napkin, not your sleeve!" "Quit kicking your brother's seat at the table!" Words of wisdom imparted by parents everywhere from time immemorial.

In high school, these lessons were conveniently tossed aside whenever a chance for a food fight arose; whenever someone had breaking news and only a few moments to spread it around while simultaneously downing a slice of pizza and a soda; or whenever someone just felt like grabbing someone else's key lime pie right off the tray. It was as though during moments like these none of us remembered our parents' most revered, and repeated, lesson on manners: "What, were you raised by wolves?"

Yet, the telltale signs of inelegance still abound in the adult workplace. There's the ill-manneredness of the colleague who pulls out a toothpick at the table immediately after finishing lunch. The co-worker who intercepts you as you step off the elevator in the morning and starts bombarding you with questions before you have a chance to peel off your coat and pour a cup of coffee. The boss or co-worker who screams out down the hall, "Hey, Shelly, come here! *SHEL-LEEEEEEEE!*" The insensitivity of the office mate who indiscriminately gossips in detail about how so-and-so broke down and cried right in front of the whole office when served with divorce papers.

Certainly, the above examples vie for runner-up in the Emily Post Bad Manners contest. But first place goes to those who are cutting-edge tech savvy but living in the Stone Age when it comes to etiquette. It's the equivalent to being "dissed" in school in front of all your high school friends. In the workplace the diss is delivered by those who disregard their co-workers by not shutting off their pagers and phones during meetings, or by continuing to read their e-mails and to take phone calls in the midst of a discussion in their office.

When you forgot to write your grandparents a thank-you note for your birthday gift, you got off easy with a scolding. When you neglected to tell your parents your biology teacher wanted to talk with them, you rated being grounded. And when you threw your lunch at a classmate, you found yourself in detention. Today, eating your salad with the wrong fork at an important company function may—or may not—bring consequences. But leave your cell phone on during the sales conference, fall asleep during the staff meeting, or roll your eyes in boredom when the boss is looking, and you may end up with a stalled career.

Lesson: While good manners are not a guarantee you'll get ahead, bad manners most assuredly will hold you back. Best to watch your P's and Q's.

RISK TAKING

Teens are notorious for assuming high levels of risk. Only a group of seventeen-year-olds would have the nerve, *or stupidity*, to high-dive off the roof of a suburban house into a ten-foot-deep backyard swimming pool. (If the 177-pounder had been six pounds heavier, he would have suffered a broken neck on impact.) For teen risk takers, the mixture of courage and inexperience can be either a wildly intoxicating or potentially deadly cocktail. Or both.

Parents and teachers warn and worry about risk, but they often fail to acknowledge the second half of the equation: reward. The weakling who takes on the school bully and wins becomes a hero. When the teenager whose parents are out of town hosts four hundred classmates at the parents' house—*and doesn't get caught*—she earns major points with friends new and old.

One of the most important skills we learn in high school, and bring with us to the workplace years later, is the ability (or inability) to assess risk—to differentiate between the big and the small risk, the smart and the dumb risk.

Every day in the workplace we are presented with risks and rewards. The dumb risks are usually obvious. People generally have a pretty good idea about what will get them fired or get their company sued. And *most* of us have enough sense to back off before doing real harm.

Successful people learn to identify and take small risks, then escalate gradually. In high school you were savvy enough to learn mom and dad's and the teachers' boundaries. If curfew was 10:00 P.M., you tested the waters by coming home at 10:15 P.M.—not 3:30 the next morning. The same rules apply at work: small risks first.

Of course, people who take risks invariably make mistakes. In high school and in the workplace, some try to lie their way out of it. This is a short-term strategy with long-term strategy repercussions. It may work once or twice, but eventually you'll be exposed. Once you are, your credibility is destroyed.

The savviest teens are the ones who are honest and forthright with their parents. "Mom, I screwed up. I dented the front bumper of the car in the drive-through at McDonald's. I could make up a long, sad story, but the truth is I should have been watching the road but I was changing the radio station. If you want to tell me that what I did was really stupid and dangerous, I will agree with you. I will also promise to be more careful in the future. I will do whatever you need me to do to pay for the damage." Odds are, the parents' anger came and went in a flash, and *they* paid for the repairs.

Similarly, the best time to report a mistake at work to the boss is as early as possible, even if you're not completely certain you made one. "Boss, I'm not certain, but I may have gotten in over my head on the KAMA project. I'm over budget. Here's a summary of the situation as I see it and three options I've identified for how to fix the problem. I accept full responsibility. For now, though, I want to see if you agree with my assessment and need to ask for your guidance on how to stop the financial bleeding."

Most bosses respond well to this approach: you're asking them for help (which affirms that they are in charge); you are proposing solutions; you are demonstrating that you accept responsibility; and you are demonstrating that you are leadership material.

Still, you may be wondering, why take risks at all? Because in high school and at work, the people who are 100 percent risk averse are safe but stationary. It's hard to get noticed when you're hiding under a rock.

Lesson: Take smart risks and assume 100 percent responsibility for the outcome.

SEX EDUCATION

We're blushing already.

When a thousand teenagers are forced to spend five days a week together in a big cement box called high school, is it any wonder flirtations occur and sparks invariably fly? That halls of learning become halls of yearning as well? Why should it be any different a decade or so later when adults (these same once-upon-a-time teenagers) are forced to spend five days a week together in a cement box called the office?

In high school, it starts innocently enough. (Doesn't it always?) We flirt. We giggle. We wait by the locker at the end of the day. Then it escalates. We become a storm of hormones. And when the parents go out of town for the weekend . . . well, you know where this is headed. Years later at work, *we* go out of town—on a business trip, or to the industry convention. Everyone stumbles into the hotel bar at 11:30 P.M. The glazed eyes of two colleagues meet, lock and . . . "Uh-oh." Well, you know where this is headed, too.

If you need further convincing that work is really high school for grown-ups, just watch how adults behave like teenagers when it comes to sexual attraction. It's embarrassing. The stolen glances during the staff meeting, the whispers, the brushing by one another, the planning of the clandestine rendezvous.

And if these clues aren't enough, there are the e-mails. Prose styles range from sickly saccharine high school–style love poems to the shockingly explicit. If the lovebirds only knew that the invisible twenty-three-year-old information technology specialist down the hall reads their saucy "secret" exchanges every morning while gnawing on jelly doughnuts and gulping black coffee. The grin widens on the IT specialist's face when, with the devious click of a finger on the send button, their salacious secrets are forwarded to his buddies in the building.

The couples always believe they are discreet. After all, each told only one person, a trusted friend—often from work—who was *sworn* to secrecy. Yeah, right.

Will we ever learn?

Whether it's high school or the office, the impact on reputa-tions—and families—can be devastating. In both settings, the "clan-destine" couple takes enormous risks and faces dire, life-altering consequences. The breakup is almost always humiliating, melodra-matic, and public.

If right about now you are expecting us to scold you, to wag a finger at you and warn, "Don't you dare even think about it!" you're wrong. We'll leave that to your mother.

You know it is stupid. *You* know it is dangerous. You don't need us to tell you that. You know it can be career suicide to get

involved with anyone in your reporting chain, whether that someone is above or beneath you. And, if you are a dinosaur who still
calls the women you work with "hon" or "sweetie" or "doll" and
likes to pat the fanny of the person you dispatch to fetch your
coffee, you don't need this book; you need a lawyer.

Yet, despite all the risks, new romances *still* blossom daily in
workplaces everywhere. There must be good reasons why smart
people keep doing something as seemingly dumb as getting involved with people at work. What are they?

To begin with, when it's consensual, and power is not abused,
office romances can be thrilling *precisely* because they are so dangerous.

Second, if you're fishing for romance, you gotta fish where the
fish are.

Finally, while nobody wants to publicize this, a lot of office
romances have happy endings: thousands of workers meet their
future life partners at work.

> **Lesson:** Carefully weigh the risks and rewards be-
> fore getting romantically involved with someone at
> work.

VOCABULARY

Choose your words with care.

Everyone is on edge in high school. Parents and teachers find their authority challenged. Students want to express their independence and individuality. Teens, for the first time, are seeking to attract and be understood by the opposite sex. There is a tremendous amount of negotiating going on. The right language and communication skills are requisites for success in the teenage milieu. And in the workplace as well.

What is said and how it is said is critical to every worker's success. In fact, in the workplace you probably get fewer chances than you did in your school life to say, "Oh, wait a minute. That's not what I meant."

Remember those friends who could finish sentences for you? They knew exactly what was meant when you said, "Oh, sh____, this is going to put me in totally f_____ hot water." You spoke plainly then, although some of you may have flavored your talk with too many expletives. In the office, those expletives will fly back in your face, tarnishing your credibility and stature.

Another damaging vocabulary problem in the workplace is the use of jargon and overly obscure prose. Few of your colleagues, clients, or customers will take, or have, the time or energy to figure out what you were trying to say when you e-mailed, "I have the expectation that the aforementioned issue with respect to our client and about which I previously made you cognizant, will be handled with dispatch and prior to its ascension to the next level of con-flagration." Huh?

By replacing the simpler, familiar language of youth with a more pretentious style, many of us confuse and irritate colleagues and customers, slowing productivity. Instead, why not say, "We're hoping to deliver our WidgetWonders to Mason Brothers by the end of next week so we won't lose them as a customer." Ah, the clarity of plainspeak.

Get back to the basics—minus the swearing, please. Why send your colleagues to the dictionary? What impresses in the workplace is not the use of fifty-cent words and convoluted, paragraph-long sentences. What succeeds when you speak or write is getting your message across. That comes from clarity, preciseness, and brevity. What impresses even more is respecting your audience by using an even-tempered tone. Gandhi wisely, and simply, said, "When you are right, you never have to raise your voice. And when you are wrong, you can't afford to."

Lesson: "Success involves using the right word and not its second cousin," said Mark Twain. It involves omitting jargon and trash talk, and making your point clear and compelling.

GRADUATION!

"The world is your oyster. Crack it open!"

"The future awaits you. Make an indelible mark on it."

"Just do it."

High school commencement messages are almost always the same: the valedictorian first tells the class to hold on to the memories of the last four years and to go out and meet the world with open arms, open minds, open hearts. The student-body president echoes the same sentiments. Then, *before* you can release the balloons hidden under your graduation robe or throw your mortar board high in the sky, you and your proud parents hear the official commencement address offered by the president of the local bank, or the mayor of the town. They are full of congratulations and they speak with envy about the graduates' youth, energy, and promise.

They talk wistfully about wanting to be seventeen again, to get a second chance to do it all over.

We're not so sure about *that* comment. Who wants to relive four of the most turbulent, emotional, unpredictable, insecure, gawky, and occasionally humiliating years of their life? Weren't braces and breakups horrible enough the first time?

In contrast, as an adult you have more freedom, more money, and more power. Never as much as you want, of course, but more than you did in high school. You can drive the family car whenever you feel like it. You can come and go as you please. You can do all the fun adult stuff your parents told you *not* to do in high school.

And most important, you have choices.

In high school, as a student, you probably got labeled—and those labels stuck, because teenagers often lack the skills to undo their stereotyping.

But you can undo yours.

You know yourself. You know your strengths and weaknesses. You *do* have the ability to change and control your image and reputation at work.

The high school you enroll in at fourteen is generally the place, and the people, you are stuck with until age eighteen. While some kids transfer, of course, teens typically cannot decide one day in the middle of the semester that they are fed up and want to change schools.

But you can.

Adults change jobs every day. They get chances to repackage and reinvent themselves. In fact, changing departments, being asked to manage a new project, or getting a new boss may be all you need to change what others think of you.

The biggest difference between a teenager and an adult is experience. The teenager is constantly seeking, trying on new things—clothes, attitudes, friends, ideas—in search of the best fit. Teenagers don't have wisdom.

But you do.

After years of trial and error, you have a better understanding of what works for you—and what doesn't. You may not have figured out until years later that you look bad in red; that you have the ability to win people's trust; that you express yourself better in person than on paper; that people want to listen to you.

After years of trial and error, you also have a better understanding of what is true: that it hurts as much at forty as it did at sixteen when people are cruel to each other.

Along the way we hope you also have figured out that in both school and work there is and can be much good.

If you are tremendously lucky, you will, at some point in your career, work with a group of people who bring out the best in you. People who teach you the business inside and out. People you trust, admire, and even grow to love. People who grow to love and trust you. These people become your second family. They comforted you when your marriage broke up, or covered for you during those final months when your mom was dying. People you still talk to, ten years after you quit that job to go back to school, move out of state, raise a family, or change careers.

These workplaces are as magical and memorable as they are rare. If you haven't found one yet, keep looking until you do.

And you will.